"Through relatable personal stories and easy to follow action plans, Jamie Vanek's, *Buried in Business*, is an enlightening and easy to follow read for both executives and administrative professionals alike. *Buried in Business* should be a must read for executives at any level and then passed on to their administrative team to help foster true partnerships moving forward."

DEBRA COLEMAN
Executive Assistant

"What a great book! Jamie has done an amazing job of creating a great resource for entrepreneurs and business leaders to help them understand the impact and the necessity of a strong, motivated administrative team."

SHAWN KUHLE
CEO and Serial Entrepreneur

"Buried in Business helped me re-envision what efficiency looks like in our business. By clarifying roles and empowering our admin team with practical tools, our productivity has grown exponentially. Not only that, but the team feels valued for the talent and assets they bring to our company. Jamie Vanek's book is an incredible guide for anyone looking to level up their teams! I strongly recommend it!"

JOHN TRANT
Vice President of Turner Strategic Technologies, LLC

"Not only was this book a practical, easy to follow business tool, it was also a highly enjoyable read! Chalked full of helpful tips, valuable advice and relatable stories, *Buried in Business* is a must read for anyone looking to elevate their admin team and empower their employees."

BRAD SALTER
CFO

"Administration is not a support function, it is a leadership function. Vanek's thinking is dead on, raising our awareness of the word Administration to its proper place inside the Sr. Leadership Team. For years I've been describing modern healthy organizations as "self-integrating", after reading this work I will now say 'self-administering and self-integrating" teams. If I was not so wedded to the word integrator through my work at EOS® I might switch out the word integrator with administrator. As part of their seat/ job, every leader around a leadership team table owns the *role* of Administration. They are accountable for thinking about how "it" all fits together, for understanding how the entire house in Vanek's model is constructed and how it all works together. They are constantly challenging: "if we make this change how will it impact everything else?" Administration is undervalued and misunderstood, this book will bring you into the modern age and give you a correct perspective on the importance of administration in modern organizations. A great company book club solution to open the eyes and minds of your existing and up and coming leaders."

WALT BROWN
Expert Implementer™ at EOS™ Worldwide, Coach, Author

"This is a book I did not know was needed, but Jamie's refreshing take on this unsung position is as illuminating as it is entertaining."

JAMES COOK
Copywriter

"Buried in Business is a must read for any business owner wanting to optimize the often overlooked but critically essential administrative function. Using personal anecdotes and valuable advice gained from years of experience building a high functioning team, Jamie shares a practical and easy to follow model for building a successful administrative team to support a company's operations. Readers committed to success will benefit from using the Adminnovate concept to create success for their own companies."

MARY BETH GIBSON
Co-Founder and Board Member, Here for the Girls

"Jamie Vanek has such a deep passion for helping businesses make the most out of their admin. Her delivery throughout this book is straight to the point, but her heart rings true throughout each page. Vanek presents her admin model with conviction, but in such a concise manner, anyone can put her suggestions to practice. This book is full of wisdom, wit, and working tactics. A must-read for anyone looking to streamline their business while elevating their admin team: the ultimate win-win."

MARY ANNA RODABOUGH
Writer, Coach

buried
in
business

buried
in
business

find freedom by
unlocking the power of
your admin team

JAMIE VANEK

buried in business

FIND FREEDOM BY UNLOCKING THE POWER OF YOUR ADMIN TEAM

JAMIE VANEK

Published and distributed by Merack Publishing.

Library of Congress Control Number: 2022905670
Vanek, Jamie
Buried in Business: Find Freedom by Unlocking the Power of Your Admin Team

ISBN Paperback 978-1-957048-27-7
ISBN Hardcover 978-1-957048-29-1
ISBN eBook 978-1-957048-28-4

This book is dedicated to all of the administrative professionals doing the work behind the scenes and the leaders who appreciate them.

Contents

introduction

As a small business owner or manager, can you imagine being able to take a vacation and *not* check emails? Can you imagine turning your work phone off in the evenings to focus on your family? Can you imagine having a long weekend *every* weekend? Can you imagine taking a class, or doing anything, *just for fun*? This is possible, and it starts with your team.

It takes a village to grow a company. Your admin team is the village behind the business, keeping it running smoothly when you're not there. The problem is that administrators are frequently pigeonholed into support roles. Throughout my career in construction I saw this trend over and over again as the staff working behind the scenes were undervalued and lacked opportunity for growth. Your team wants to make meaningful contributions. They want to know that there's a career development path. It's time to dismantle the stigma, rethink admin structure, and restore respectability to these roles. Empowering your admin team means that you can rest easy at night knowing your company is in good hands.

I wrote this book because I believe in opportunity. My journey from art teacher to construction executive is long and winding, but I've learned many valuable lessons along the way.

This book includes intimate stories of how the trials, successes, and failures of administration have shaped my career. More importantly, it's a model that creates opportunity for you and your support team to get out of the weeds and lead more purposeful careers.

In the Beginning... I Got Fired

I'd never been fired before. I quit dozens of low stakes jobs throughout my teenage and early adult years, but I had never been fired. I was only working at Spintas & Sons for two weeks through a temporary placement agency as I contemplated a career change.

Five years prior, I graduated as valedictorian from my small art college outside Philadelphia and taught art classes in an affluent suburban elementary school. Had my fiancé not joined the US Navy, uprooted my well-planned life and relocated to Norfolk, Virginia, I may very well still be teaching sticky six year-olds how to use scissors and glue.

Before moving from Pennsylvania to Virginia, I had fulfilled my checklist:

- Get tenure at the school where I was teaching
- Finish graduate school
- Obtain teaching certifications in a variety of subjects
- Sell my condo
- Secure a new teaching position in Virginia

I was very good at planning, but I was not very good at change. My new teaching position in Virginia was a terrible fit and I submitted my resignation within five months. Everything I had studied and planned for crumbled.

What was a smart, talented artist and Navy wife to do next? I searched the web, met with career counselors, drank too much alcohol with my neighbors and finally registered with a temporary employment agency.

When I registered at the temp agency, the manager looked over my resume and was aghast that I would seek employment through them. "How do you *not* have a job, Jamie?" she asked rhetorically. Having a master's degree, a clean background and plenty of random experience, I was overqualified for most of their positions. I didn't care. After four years of teaching, where you're never really "off the clock," I just wanted to work at an office where I could punch out at the end of the day.

They placed me in the accounts payable department of Spintas & Sons, auditing invoices for fifteen dollars an hour. On my first day, the accounting manager welcomed me enthusiastically—and with the same optimistic skepticism as the temp agency. *How did I not have a job?*

I was given a fob to enter the glass-front building and placed in my cubicle among the dozens of others on the accounting floor. The room was quiet relative to the number of people who occupied the cubicles. Everyone kept their heads down and voices low. My job was tedious and thankless, scouring pages of part numbers on invoices and matching them with purchase orders. After verifying the part numbers, the next step was to obtain approval from the project managers.

What was a project manager? I'd never heard of such a position, but these project managers were mysterious and important men who had their own offices, *real offices*, on the third floor. Rather than walking the invoices to our important "co-workers," I had to call them for approval before passing the invoice along.

The project managers had the power to spend, approve and deny millions of dollars on these invoices, and were never in the office to receive my phone call. They had assistants who could speak on their behalf. I didn't know what the third floor looked like, but imagined corner offices with eight-foot high windowed walls and sleek, modern desks and assistants with smaller offices beside them—à la *Mad Men*. I wanted so badly to have that kind of power and importance. I still didn't quite know what a project manager did, but I wanted to be one.

As a temporary employee I wasn't supposed to meddle in their processes. My aspirations got the best of me. I asked too many questions. I demanded too much information. I didn't know my place. I got fired.

Admin is a Dirty Word

Fourteen years after being fired from Spintas & Sons, I sat across from the owner of a growing construction company. The plush, cream-colored chairs reclined slightly as we debated my executive title.

"Vice president of administration," he suggested.

"Absolutely not," I rebutted.

VP of administration sounds like a great title, right? The owner was a brilliant man, but he couldn't understand why I insisted he remove the last two words: *of administration.*

Administration is necessary in all businesses. However, small and medium businesses struggle to find the right structure for their administrative office staff. They are the Steady Eddy's, Reliable Rita's, and Lean-on Lisa's of the workplace. They pick up pieces behind messy managers, keep office supplies stocked, make sure everyone gets paid and, in short, "keep us all straight" behind the scenes. Admin is necessary, but it is not glamorous.

After more than a decade of experience working in the construction industry, I realized the inefficiencies that are prevalent in many companies. When I finally landed in a company who had a better approach, it was refreshing.

When I made the leap into the executive team, I did not want to be seen as the "Steady Eddy" behind the scenes. I wanted a voice. As a woman in construction, I was already passed over during conversations—assumed to be the receptionist and dismissed by old-school customers. Tacking the word *administration* to my title would only confirm the perception that the woman was the silent caretaker of the organization.

The discomfort that I felt around the word *admin* is what inspired me to write this book. Why is admin such a dirty word? Where did it lose its respectability and—more importantly—how do we get it back?

Why You Should Read This Book

Whether you are a business owner or in middle management, understanding how the admin functions serve as a pipeline for talent will help you rethink your approach to your next hire or promotion. Whether you need to add to your admin team, refine roles or get more from your current staff, this book will provide tools to level up your administrative team from being "just admin" to being your **A-team**.

We're going to dive into unrealized potential within your company. Simon Sinek, one of the most-watched TED Talk presenters, does an excellent job illustrating the difference between people with authority and leaders. If you are the boss, you have the authority to make decisions and direct employees to perform tasks. A boss who leads with authority has a team who performs tasks, and if that boss is lucky, no one will quit. If you're the leader, your impact is more significant than just having a gainfully employed team. It's easy to have authority over your administrative team, but if you want to elevate your team, you must read this book from a leader's perspective.

Do you want a team who chugs along under your authority, or do you want to lead a group of people who are inspired?

Do you want your staff to blindly perform tasks, or bring new ideas to the table?

Do you want your team to follow your commands, or fulfill your vision?

Leaders have teams that support them and collaborate to propel them to success. As a great leader, you need to recognize the power that surrounds you. You should become an expert—not just of your subject matter—but of your team. This book will create clarity within the team, and identify opportunities for growth that will elevate both your team and your company. **It's time to stand in your greatness as a person who has the power to change how we do business.**

After reading this book you will have a powerful and easy-to-use tool to level up your admin team. Before we get to the Adminnovate Model, it's important that you understand the framework for analyzing the administrative roles within your company. Chapters one through nine will give you a solid framework for viewing the roles and tools within your organization. By first creating clarity and vision, you can more effectively use the Adminnovate Model to solve your most pressing admin issues.

Experts

I've come a long way in my career, from a fifteen-year-old girl on the Jersey boardwalk taking tickets for rides, to being an executive at a $100 million private company before the age of forty. It's a strange and winding path, but I've gathered a book of lessons along the way to share what great companies, and great mentors, do well.

There are many experts in leadership that I admire like Brené Brown, Adam Grant, Steven Covey and Jim Collins. They have earned the degrees, done the research, guided leadership teams in Fortune 500 companies, and will be regarded as experts in their fields for years to come. They have done the hard work to give us evidence-based tools to use in our own leadership situations to improve our impact on our companies, families, employees, and coworkers. If that's what you're looking for, I recommend you buy their books in addition to mine.

This book is filled with relatable stories from inside the world of administration and provides tactical tools to answer your most pressing admin issues. If you're interested in finding clarity, efficiency, and opportunity within your organization then read on, my friend.

CHAPTER 1

the adminnovate model

Finding My Place

Accepting a job offer after a single phone interview is a terrible idea. I found myself at an underfunded middle school in Virginia, teaching thirteen teens with special needs with very little support. It felt unfair to these children that they were taught by a woman who held the right credentials, but wasn't passionate about teaching. I lasted only six months before I quit. I found myself in a new marriage, in a new state, and with no job. My quarter-life crisis hit hard.

I was well-qualified, but only for a handful of careers that I was ready to abandon. Searching the internet and meeting with career counselors when I had no clear direction was exasperating. I was convinced that there was something I was born to do, I just hadn't found it. At the ripe age of twenty-seven, I was out of energy for more soul searching. I gave up and handed over my career prospects to a temporary employment agency so they could market me in a pretty little overqualified package. Little did I know that returning to an entry-level position would help me discover the industry where I belonged: construction.

Construction careers don't run in my family. There isn't a legacy of electricians or family businesses to follow. However, in the bedroom where I grew up I had an elegant dollhouse. This wasn't your ordinary dollhouse. It was a complete house with sides that hinged open to reveal a detailed interior. The rooms and stairs were laid out like a real house, not like the backless playhouses you'd find in a toy store. The ceilings and floors had hollow spaces between the layers to run electricity. It towered three stories, with large pillars on the front porch that reminded me of colonial mansions. It was engineered and carefully crafted by my dad after my parents got married. I love the story of how he built it, borrowing library books, and using pieces of old fruit crates to construct the house. I grew up admiring what it stood for: resourcefulness, structure, and creation.

Education offered stability and the chance to make the world a better place. However, construction brought satisfaction from the completion of a project and had immense potential for career growth. The problem was that I lacked the credibility to enter the world of construction at a higher level. As years went by, I worked at two different construction companies, holding various positions, but I was always the assistant. I craved more. My passion was in construction, but I was ready to move up the career ladder in the industry.

What's in a Name?

Contract administrator sounded a whole lot better than being anyone's assistant. Ten years into my contrasting career of education and construction I'd been a teacher, a preschool director, a project manager assistant, and an assistant project manager. In education I'd held positions of authority (granted, my authority was over children). But when it came to construction, the term "assistant" was always tagged on to my title. When I found the opportunity to be a contract administrator, it was a refreshing change. I applied for a job in construction that was not an assistant of anything.

In 2013 I joined Hestel Construction as a contract administrator. It wasn't the new and exciting career I was looking for, but it was a new opportunity that wasn't labeled as an "assistant."

This type of administrative role is prevalent but is commonly titled as an assistant. The assistant's job is to process any amount of administrative paperwork that is required by a project: keeping files organized, logging data, populating contract templates, ordering bonds and insurance, reviewing documents for compliance, and verifying invoices. The admin keeps tabs on the project manager (PM) and answers for them in their absence. It requires following prescribed processes and picking up any paperwork in the wake of the busy and important PM.

This new company treated their admin staff differently than your typical construction company. The main difference was the title, contract admin, and the self-sufficiency of the PMs. The contract admin was not an assistant. The PMs managed their own files and prepared their own documents instead of passing them off to an assistant. And guess what? The PMs were perfectly capable of keeping their projects organized. Who knew?

There were many things that made Hestel Construction progressive and one of the best places I've ever worked, but the very first impression was the change in title. Coming from someone who aspired to be a project manager and had no interest in being anyone's assistant, I was instantly grateful for the contract administrator title compared to being called an assistant. It carried a different air of importance, regardless of the similarities in qualifications.

You Can Change Anything

When I was hired, Hestel Construction was still very small, and they were growing their federal contracting capabilities. I was the sole contract administrator (CA).

The CA's role was **not** to keep the PMs in check, it was to be a liaison between operations and accounting, mitigating risk and assuring positive project cash flow. This slight shift in purpose made all the difference in being seen as a "catch-all" for the higher paid PMs and being a respected contributor to the projects.

My first week was filled with self-guided research of their projects and processes. As I sifted through their files, I came across Excel documents that were long, cumbersome, and prone to errors.

"Jim, are you set on using this spreadsheet or can I create one that is more user-friendly?" I asked.

"You can change anything that makes sense for what you need to do," he responded.

It sounded so simple, but this was the first time any supervisor had given me permission to change a tool they had been using for years. *And he didn't even think twice about it.* It was as if a whole new world opened up to me with the single phrase *you can change anything*.

Growth

Jim, as the vice president of construction, gave me full reign to change any internal process that came across my desk, and to cross-train with any department that I could fit into my schedule. The autonomy was glorious! The freedom gave me space to work closely with project managers, learn the accounting system and assist with other basic functions in the company.

Jim did not command with authority, he led with confidence. He knew that he'd hired the right people, and that he could trust his team to perform without being micromanaged. His door was always open, and no issue was too big or small to brainstorm with him. If you came to him with the passion to do what was right, no mistake was unfixable. Over the years, Jim became a close mentor and friend.

At Hestel Construction, I was given the freedom to experiment, learn, try and fail. The culture of the company and the mindset of my mentor provided tremendous opportunities for growth. Had I stayed in my contract admin box, going through the motions without question, my trajectory would have looked a lot different. I felt empowered to make changes and explore new ways of doing business.

Instead of staying in a stagnant admin role, I was promoted to project manager in year one. When the company landed a $4 million contract, I was first in line to manage the new customer. I excelled at project management and trained my contract admin replacement. A self-studied and curious PM,

I obtained my Project Management Professional certification and was awarded project manager of the year by our regional association in 2018. This is where I belonged. To finally discover and achieve what I had glimpsed at Spintas & Sons years ago was profoundly satisfying. Shortly after I was promoted to joint venture program manager, managing multi-million-dollar contracts across the United States. Seven years after being hired as a CA, I was promoted to vice president of Hestel Construction. Two short years later, I became president of its sister company.

It wasn't just my curiosity and career that grew. Over the same nine-year span, the company experienced exponential growth and benefitted from my understanding of the inner workings of every department at Hestel Construction. The company, as a whole, went from a single office of thirteen people to a company of more than 250 with ten locations across the United States. This explosive growth led to numerous promotions for internal team members.

The Number One Reason

Whether it's the chance to explore new roles and ideas, or a pathway for linear advancement, opportunity is the key to keeping A-players engaged. In a 2006 Gallup poll regarding employee turnover, the number one reason people cited for leaving a company was for career advancement and promotional opportunities.[1] More than ten years later, the trend remains. In 2017, the Society for Human Resource Management (SHRM) also reported the primary reason people leave jobs is for career development.[2]

While the classic notion of structure and process is important in business, we also need to leave room for exploration, innovation and growth from the bottom levels to the top. Just like my first few years at Hestel Construction, leaving room for autonomy and self-guided learning has benefits for the individual and the company. If you continue to follow processes simply because that's the way you've always done them, you and your team are missing opportunities for improvement in your processes, structure, and personnel.

How do you maintain structure and clarity while still providing opportunity for learning and growth in administration? At Hestel Construction, there were several characteristics that made it a great place to create efficiencies and see growth:

- Their approach to hiring
- Being able to define specific workflows
- Offering a descriptive title and specific purpose
- Having the authority to make changes

---

1   Robison, Jennifer, "Turning Around Employee Turnover," Gallup, May 8, 2008, https://news.gallup.com/businessjournal/106912/turning-around-your-turnover-problem.aspx.

2   Tarallo, Mark, "How to Reduce Employee Turnover Through Robust Retention Strategies," SHRM, September 17, 2018, https://www.shrm.org/resourcesandtools/hr-topics/talent-acquisition/pages/how-to-reduce-employee-turnover-through-robust-retention-strategies.aspx.

- Having a personal and cultural fit
- Offering the opportunity to learn
- Providing mentorship

I've had the privilege to work with phenomenal mentors and coaches. I've benefited from great leaders who paved the way for my success and supported my growth. I believe that everyone deserves the same level of opportunity that I have experienced. This is why I want to share my experience with you. You too can have the kind of impact on your team that my mentors had on me. It starts with you.

How Did We Get Here?

Small businesses (fewer than 500 employees) make up 99.9% of businesses in the United States and employ over 47% of the workforce. However, 81% of administrative professionals work in companies with over 500 employees.[3] This doesn't add up. Where does that leave small business owners who are in need of administrative support?

Small business owners find themselves scrambling to get help, turning to any available option to get things done. They do it themselves, lean on friends and family, and hire inexperienced people. Things get messy—even a little scrappy. This might work in the early years of the company when resources are limited. But as the company grows, these early tactics become

---

3   Zippia, "Administrative Professional Statistics and Facts in the US," accessed 8 March 2022, https://www.zippia.com/administrative-professional-jobs/demographics/.

irrelevant and can hold the company back—making the administrative burden feel like, well, a *burden*.

My model for administrative support will help you evolve from the early tactics of growing your business. It will let you break free from the administrative burden, and empower your team to lift you to the next level.

The Adminnovate Model

I recently went on a rafting trip with my husband and children through the Shenandoah mountains. Armed with our life vests, oars, and peanut butter and jelly sandwiches, we spent five hours paddling, swimming and drifting down the river. When the river slowed and we floated lazily through the water, we admired the houses perched on the sides of the river, up steep riverbanks and on distant mountain sides. These were not cookie-cutter houses built in a day by a common developer. These houses were customized, with expansive windows and balconies to take in the scenic river views. However, there was a common theme among these beautiful homes; they were all variants of an A-frame house.

The basic elements of an A-frame house are simple and strong. It has a stable base, holds its shape, and withstands snow and rain. Following the notion of simple and strong, my goal is to help you build a high performing admin team like an A-frame house through the Adminnovate Model. There are two structures that make up the Adminnovate Model: the Adminnovate Model House (we will refer to as the AM House) and the Adminnivate Model Village (we will refer to as the AM Village). The AM House starts with a wide foundation where you will take inventory of your people and processes. The AM Village brings your houses together to ensure each role has proper connections and collaboration within the company. Using supporting information, I will guide you through its construction in a way that will lead you to effective administrative resolutions. You will be guided through the process of evolving your admin team from being "just admin" to being a high-performing A-team.

Enter the House

To enter a house, you start at the front door, which is often used as a metaphor to symbolize opportunity. *When one door closes another opens.* Think of your administrative staff opening a door to enter your organization. When they enter their role in your company, imagine them entering a house designed especially for their role. When they enter, what does the house look like? Does it have a clear and respectable purpose that contributes to moving the company forward? Is it so chaotic that it's hard to make sense of its purpose, with information flying in every direction?

Maybe your admin roles are not chaotic, but we are going to hone them to define their purpose and opportunities. In the first several chapters of this book we will equate characteristics of your administrative roles to elements of a house. Think about each administrative person in your company operating in a separate house. There is a door through which they enter, and through which they will eventually leave if the environment is not efficient, effective, or enjoyable.

The first consideration is the entry door. The entry/exit door never goes away. This is how they are welcomed into the company and how they exit the company. This is the first misconception for leaders. Even if you have a staff member who has been with you for ten, twenty or thirty years, that exit door is always there. Whether it's a voluntary resignation, retirement, or they get hit by the proverbial bus—the reality is they can leave through this door at any time. You do not want to walk into your office one day to find out your office manager of twenty years has resigned.

You want to create a team where people stay. You want to create a village where houses are connected, maintained, and not abandoned. However, leaving an admin person in a stagnant house that never changes will either push them out of the organization or lead to breakdowns in productivity and efficiency. A tenured employee who stays in a house that never changes continues doing the same things "because that's the way we've always done them."

Think of it like your house. If you don't do some basic maintenance and occasional upgrades, the house deteriorates over time. At a minimum, you keep it clean, patch leaky roofs, and change the occasional air filter to keep the major systems running efficiently. However, most homeowners put additional TLC into their homes over time: upgrading kitchens, building decks, and replacing appliances. An admin who doesn't keep their processes maintained and whose boss doesn't provide resources for upgrades will eventually be in a run-down, outdated, and inefficient role.

Through this book we'll analyze the structure of the Adminnovate Model and how you can implement it in your business. We'll also identify key opportunities for maintenance and upgrades. Let's take a look around the Adminnovate Model House. There are seven key elements of the AM House:

1. The Front Door = Hiring & Firing (or resignation)
2. Windows = Workflows
3. The Address = Title & Purpose
4. The Deed = Ownership & Authority
5. The Thermostat = Personal Fit
6. New Doors = Opportunity
7. Bracing = Mentoring

Chances are you haven't given each of these characteristics a lot of thought for your admin roles. You may have relied on hunches, past experience, or standard practices to hire & manage your admin staff. You may have hired someone for a role years ago, and as the company has evolved, the role has stayed the same. As we step through each element of the AM House in this book, you will gain insights and learn new ways to define and refine your AM Houses. Don't worry about memorizing this list. We'll step through each element one at a time.

Rooms without Doors

Offering career advancement isn't always about money, it's about opportunities to learn and grow, earn respect and authority. At the end of the day, everyone in the company wants to feel valued. Working in a stagnant one-room house prevents growth and tends to make someone feel unappreciated. Offering opportunities for learning is like building new rooms for your admin team—and occasionally providing keys to a new house.

The operations side of construction has a solid model for growth. Someone can enter the field doing basic labor, then learn a trade and eventually become a foreman, supervisor or superintendent. In project management the path typically starts with project engineer, then assistant project manager, and up to different levels of project management. Each step on the promotion scale is like a new door opening to the next room.

The problem is that the administrative rooms in small businesses typically do not have clearly defined doors other than the entry/exit door. These rooms without doors pigeonhole your admin people into small areas without room for growth. When they start looking for growth, if the only door available is the entry/exit door, guess where they will go.

What is the next step for an administrative assistant? Will there ever be an opportunity for them to fill the role of their current boss? There is often a great disparity between an entry-level admin and their supervisor's role—which is not easily bridged. In smaller companies and startups, this disparity is even wider, with the admin often reporting directly to the owner or upper-level management. This leaves the admin in a one-room, messy house, leading to lower career development and higher turnover.

There are just under three and a half million secretaries and administrative assistants in the United States.[4] That's three million too many. Why? I've read through hundreds of resumes with "administrative assistant" listed under prior experience. This becomes a problem when the specific duties and responsibilities vary greatly, even with a common title. The generic title of administrative assistant lends itself to inconsistent interpretation because there is no real meaning behind it.

I was an administrative assistant at the age of sixteen, and my only responsibility was to alphabetize receipts at a car dealership. This undermines the value of career administrative assistants who take on more significant responsibilities. There are appropriate and valuable places for administrative assistants, but over three million gives me reason for concern that *millions of employees* in thousands of companies will not have clear avenues for growth.

---

4   Occupational Outlook Handbook, "Secretaries and Administrative Assistants," Bureau of Labor Statistics, U.S. Department of Labor, Accessed February 22, 2022, https://www.bls.gov/ooh/office-and-administrative-support/secretaries-and-administrative-assistants.htm.

What if your company doesn't have a clear promotional structure for its admin staff or your employee isn't ready to move up? Opportunity doesn't have to come in the form of a promotion. Feeling valued and developed in an admin role can come in the form of authority, innovation, or mentorship.

We will explore ways to define the AM Houses, identify the different features of the house that will make roles clearer, and create opportunities for learning, authority and growth. While it may seem like we're putting people in boxes, it's quite the opposite. It will feel like building spaces where information continually flows in and out, admin staff are given the tools to build, and walls shift with the needs of the company. It's taking the people who are already in boxes and creating openings for them to step into their highest and best talents.

Opportunity is Everything

On September 11, 2001, we all watched in horror as the towers fell. The economic ripple effect of that tragic day eventually spread to my family, and my dad was laid off after a thirty-year career. I was in college and renting a house in northern Philadelphia with five other waiters and waitresses. My parents paid for my housing as I maintained a scholarship for tuition. While they never asked me to cover my own expenses, I could not accept their rent checks after my dad lost his job. Without further discussion, I immediately picked up an additional shift waitressing and searched for other job opportunities.

I found an opportunity with Darlene, the director of student services at my college. She embraced my determination and created a position for me with a meager wage and random office tasks, including revamping an office space for Dr. Morris, an intellectual and philosophical professor. With a fifty dollar budget, artistic license, and a directory of thrift stores, I transformed the small musty space into an eclectic old world kingdom. The stretched fabric of an umbrella displaying a vintage map hung from the ceiling. Painted across the longest wall was the professor's favorite philosophical quote. A high-backed upholstered chair, adequately nick-named *the throne*, sat in front of a cheap antique desk. This made-up administrative job was my first taste of business opportunity.

More importantly this position gave me dedicated time with a true genius. Dr. Morris was a progressive and philosophical historian who held me to a higher standard than anyone I'd ever met. The time I spent with him during my self-created employment made me feel like anything was possible. It was the kind of inspiration that only a twenty-one-year-old about to graduate college could embrace with unwavering confidence.

Finding Inspiration

More people entering the workforce need leaders who will remove traditional binds to hire, promote and lead in unexpected ways. I had the privilege of working with some inspiring and empowering leaders who challenged limiting beliefs and gave me the space to try and fail without being a failure. I had mentors who saw something in me that propelled me towards goals I would not have set for myself without their guidance. And I want you to be that person for someone else.

This isn't a conventional book about leadership; it's about dismantling the stigmas around administration and restoring respectability to create stronger infrastructure for your business. By stepping through the seven elements of the AM House, you will begin to visualize the impacts of each element on your team and your business. We will strip away the outdated ways of thinking about administration and put new structures in place. You will learn from intimate stories of trials, failures, and successes. Most importantly, you will walk away with tangible practices to unlock the power of your admin team. Let's get started.

Next Step: How to Use Appendix A

As you learn about each element of the Adminnovate Model, you will have opportunities to put the concepts into practice and begin building and refining your admin team. At the end of each chapter, you will find a **Next Step** section that will give you practical tips and exercises. These are intended to take only a few minutes of your time and to build on each other throughout the book. By the end of the book, you will be able to diagram a unique AM House and AM Village in your company and use the Adminnovate Model for future growth.

My goal is to make this as easy as possible for you. The Appendix has simple diagrams, so you don't have to be an engineer to draft a blueprint. It also downloadable if you decide to start over or want to diagram more than one AM House. This book is for you, so don't worry about making it perfect. You don't have to share it with anyone. Abandon perfectionism as you step through the exercises. Your diagrams will not be perfect or lead to life-altering epiphanies. There is no pressure here. The goal is to have you practice the diagram in a safe place so that you can use it more comfortably in the future as you work through growth and changes.

If you are the type of person who doesn't like to write in books, I've also provided a diagram that you can download at jamievanek.com/bonuses. I recommend printing the diagram to write and draw directly on it. I come from an art school and there's nothing quite like putting pencil to paper. For you techy people, by all means, complete the exercises digitally. The symbols are provided as an easy copy and paste tool.

There are two ways to approach the exercises. They are written with the intention that you will pause at the end of each chapter to reflect and practice the concept. As a former teacher, I recommend doing the exercise while the concept is fresh. However, as a businesswoman, I also recognize that your time is valuable and you may not have the luxury or desire to stop after each chapter for an exercise. You can read the book straight through, then drop back to complete each of the exercises in succession. If you choose to do the exercises after reading the book, feel free to skip the Next Step sections at the end of each chapter. They are clearly labeled so that you can come back to them at a later date and run through the exercises as many times as you like.

Whichever way you decide to use the exercises, flip to Appendix A or download the diagram at jamievanek.com/ bonuses and take a few minutes to look it over. Get familiar with the layout so when it's time to practice, you can jump in with little hesitation. Resist the urge to start diagraming yet. Have patience, we'll walk through it together.

CHAPTER 2

the front door

A House is a Home

While exploring my post-teaching career options in 2007, the employment agency found another administrative position for me, this time with lower expectations and lower pay. I was placed as a temporary receptionist at a small construction company while the current receptionist took a medical leave of absence.

Mattesse Group's office looked like a small rancher house from the outside. In fact, it was a house, but it had been converted to an office for a small electrical construction company. The living room served as a reception area with a large L-shaped desk. The kitchen and bathroom remained domestic with residential appliances and personal décor, including a floral curtain covering the unused shower. Each of the other rooms were converted to office spaces that still smelled like Yankee Candles. It was cozy and inviting—a stark contrast to the all-glass building of Spintas & Sons.

It was a relief to enter an organization where staff from each department could stroll into each other's offices for a chat. At Mattesse Group, people were people, not robots plowing through tasks. They knew each other's families and exchanged gifts on holidays. I felt a sense of belonging that I'd missed at other companies.

Temporary receptionist was not my dream job, but I found a home in that little rancher house. From the admins to the project managers to the owner, everyone was welcoming. When I got bored at the L-shaped desk, I was free to wander around the house and ask questions of anyone who had a few spare minutes to share their knowledge. I absorbed it all, and when the receptionist recovered from surgery and my assignment was over, Carla, the owner, offered me a permanent position as a project manager assistant (PMA).

Seeing Potential

Carla was not planning to hire another admin. They did not place an ad for a job opening and didn't even have an office ready for me. They already had two tenured PMAs. At this point in my career, I had zero experience in construction or project management, but Carla saw the growth in her company and the potential in me. Instead of allowing me to leave the company through the same door I entered, she created an opportunity for me to step further into Mattesse Group's rooms.

Typical of a small construction company, there was no formal training for a new admin person at Mattesse Group. I was given a makeshift desk in the converted garage, catty-corner to the other PMAs. They eased me into the position by training me on one topic at a time. I watched everything they did and asked a zillion questions.

"What's the difference between a transmittal, a submittal and a submittal transmittal?"

They laughed at the absurdity of the words. Though they understood the content of the question, they'd never been asked to explain something so innate to their role. Everything was foreign to me, but learning was in my blood. I was ready to absorb any information I could get.

Within the next year the company expanded to a real office space where I finally stepped over a physical threshold and entered my room, the room where my career in construction would truly begin to take shape.

Lessons Learned

There are both scary and exciting elements to entering a brand-new company or career. I stumbled into Mattesse Group's door by chance, but there was something charming and inviting about their rancher house. What I saw there that enticed me to stay was their ability to adapt. The small business environment is a wonderful place for a new admin to learn and grow because there aren't corporate hoops to jump through. Small businesses start in garages, kitchens and home offices. Inviting someone new into your small businesses is like inviting a guest to dinner. It's intimate and gives you the choice of just how much cake to serve. Mattesse Group saw a match between the potential in me and the need within the growing company. They kept their minds open and the team flexible.

The Entry & Exit Door

The door to the AM House is the means through which you will gain or lose your A-players. When you're looking for the right person, internally or externally, they will be crossing an important threshold into a new role. This should not be taken lightly. As qualified as any person may be, leadership's responsibility is to set them up for success in the unique culture and demands of the company. To quote Peter Drucker (author of numerous leadership books including *The Effective Executive*), "Leadership is lifting a person's vision to higher sights, the raising of a person's performance to a higher standard, the building of a personality beyond its normal limitations." As the leader in your company, you must align your team with your vision.

The same door they enter can also become the door through which they exit, voluntarily or involuntarily. Revolving doors are expensive. According to SHRM, it costs a company an average of four thousand dollars per hire.[5] Having to replace a forty-thousand dollar employee three times in a year increases that cost to fifty-two thousand dollars. Getting and keeping the right people takes time and money but building and keeping a high performance admin team will give you a return on your investment. Following the Adminnovate Model creates efficiencies and clarity, requiring less time and fewer resources from you. With an A-team in place, you can break free from the administrative burden, focus on growing the business or simply take a break. The Adminnovate Model makes the process of backing away easy and painless. Less stress, fewer headaches, more growth.

> With the right team in place, you can break free from the administrative burden, focus on growing the business, or simply take a break.

Identifying the Need

Crossing the initial threshold into your organization is an opportunity to set expectations. Mattesse Group did not advertise for the PMA position I filled. Instead, they used my temporary placement as an extended "interview" and

---

5   SHRM Online Staff, "SHRM Benchmarking Report: $4,129 Average Cost-per-Hire," Society for Human Resource Management, August 8, 2016, https://www.shrm.org/hr-today/news/hr-news/pages/shrm-benchmarking-report-$4,100-average-cost-per-hire.aspx.

determined I would be a good fit. But not everyone has the privilege of hiring a temporary employee to see if they could fill a position. Most hiring processes start with a pressing need within the company.

"Our bookkeeper is working sixty hours a week. We need another bookkeeper."

"If I had an assistant, I could spend more time doing the important things."

"Mary quit. We need another admin."

"We need someone to update our social media."

And my favorite: "We need someone to do all the dumb shit." Yes, I have actually heard someone say this.

Because you're reading this book, you're thinking ahead. You would never say you want people to do "dumb shit." But just knowing that you need to hire an admin person is the easy part.

During the hiring process, let's first think about our approach to finding the right people and setting them up for success. (We will get to details like titles, salary and job descriptions later in the book.) No matter which position you're filling, the mindset for the team is the same. Channel your inner Jim Collins (author of *Built to Last* and *Good to Great*) and make sure you get the right people on the bus, or in our case, in the house. Before you jump into the job description, let's focus on the qualities of the people you want to attract to your team.

Missing Pieces

You cannot manifest the perfect candidate for your job opening. As hard as we try to imagine and describe the right person by writing a detailed job description, we cannot make them appear. We tend to write job descriptions with the best intentions to capture everything a candidate must possess or experience in order to be eligible for a position. We ruminate over task lists, debate titles, and become very precise in refining the qualifications. We ask for a specific number of years of experience and competence with our selected software. However, even the best recruiters cannot find the single perfect person for an opportunity—even when they come pretty darned close. A job description is a wish list, and our wish lists are flawed.

Consider the following:

- Most administrative positions are filled by women.[6]
- Women apply for positions for which they meet 100% of the criteria.[7]

---

6   "Labor Force Statistics from the Current Population Survey," U.S. Bureau of Labor Statistics, January 20, 2022, https://www.bls.gov/cps/cpsaat11.htm.

7   Mohr, Tara Sophia, "Why Women Don't Apply for Jobs Unless They're 100% Qualified," Harvard Business Review, August 25, 2014, https://hbr.org/2014/08/why-women-dont-apply-for-jobs-unless-theyre-100-qualified.

According to these stats, we are missing a huge applicant pool if we craft our requirements too tightly. Unconscious biases, stringent requirements, and lengthy wish lists that try to capture everything—instead of just the right things—will narrow your audience.

When there is an opening on your team, the tendency is to define this opening as precisely as possible. It is the missing puzzle piece with distinct shapes and edges. At this point, we will either spin our wheels searching the abyss for a perfect fit or settle for a candidate who comes close enough to jam into the empty space.

The problem is that there is nothing rigid about building teams. Building your team is not a puzzle to be solved or a predetermined shape to be filled. Your team is malleable, an evolving ball of clay, not a jigsaw puzzle. Every person who interacts with the team has the ability to mold and reshape it. The team whirls with the colors of different personalities, making it a lumpy, swirly shapeshifter. Small businesses experience this to a higher degree because the influence each person has is relatively larger compared to the whole. When adding a new piece to the ball of clay, the new part must be compatible material, but it can come in almost any shape or color. This mixture will bring new life to the group. A new member must be able to integrate into the team while contributing their unique abilities and ultimately helping the clay form and function as a vital part of the company.

Whether you're promoting from within, outsourcing, or hiring someone new, approach the missing piece as something moldable and integral to the team. This person should not be hired or promoted to fill a void; they are adding value to an already formed team.

Hire or Promote?

Before deciding if you need to hire someone new, take a look around your organization. Is there someone who fits with your company culture and has the capacity to learn the skills needed for this role? My jump from temporary receptionist to project manager assistant is the perfect example of hiring for attitude and training for aptitude. I did not possess the subject matter knowledge or skills prior to stepping into the role of PMA but had the potential and core values of the company. This helped me fit with the team and learn the workflows.

Providing opportunities for career development is one of the most important ways to retain key employees. Keep an open mind when trying to fill a new role. Lateral moves can be as effective in team building as promotions. Everyone wants to be valued. Filling a new role is an easy way to recognize your A-players, give them an avenue to learn new skills, and upgrade your team. This can be doubly beneficial if the existing team member's previous role is easier to fill than the new role.

For example, Hestel Construction was seeking a Customer Service Manager. This position required attention to detail, the ability to work in a fast-paced environment, and a high level of professionalism. These are all qualities of a high-functioning admin person. Lisa was one of our top performing bookkeepers. She learned quickly, worked quickly and was always willing to help. By offering the customer service manager position to Lisa, she was able to learn new skills, work with a new team, and created an opening for a new bookkeeper—where applicants were plentiful. The benefits to the company were obvious: the customer service manager position was filled with a vetted and tenured employee, and hiring a new bookkeeper required fewer resources than finding a new customer service manager. The benefit to Lisa was the best part—while it did not give her an instant increase in salary, it gave her the opportunity to use her skills in a new environment and quickly led to a promotion.

As we explore the seven elements of the house, take inventory of your current team. Shifting roles may become more apparent to you as you make adjustments and reshape your admin team. As a former teacher I will not lecture you on how everyone is teachable if you *just believe* in your trainee. We're running businesses. Not everyone can do any job.

> **Take careful inventory of who is on your team and whether their strengths align with the new administrative role.**

High Stakes

When it's time to hire, how do we get the right people in the door?

At Hestel Construction, Jim and I were interviewing a candidate for an entry-level position. We were not expecting the applicants to have much experience but were seeking a good culture fit—a positive attitude, attention to detail, and an eagerness to learn. We walked down the hall together, confident we were on the same page. Our third candidate waited patiently in a leather chair in the lobby, dressed in a modest but professional blue suit, notebook in hand. As we approached him, he stood and looked each of us in the eye with an outstretched hand.

"It's nice to meet you," he said with a broad smile.

We conducted the interview just as we had the previous two candidates, briefing him on our company history and culture, followed by typical interview questions. He appeared attentive, eager to please, and forthcoming with his experience. When we asked about his hobbies and interests to get a better impression of the person we may hire, he responded with swimming and fishing. Such wholesome activities!

As we departed from the conference room, Jim commented "I really liked him."

"Really? I was not impressed. Something about him seemed off." I countered.

I was puzzled. We sat in the same interview. We each shook his hand and witnessed the same responses to our questions. How could we have such contradictory opinions of the young man? We had differing gut feelings about this candidate and argued our evidence. Frustrated and unable to convince the other of our viewpoints, we brought in an objective manager. As we each pleaded our case to hire or not hire the young man, the objective manager did a quick social media search. Young people entering the workforce are advised to keep their online presence private—our candidate had not learned this important lesson. Within a few minutes, the other manager found some questionable photos and Twitter posts that supported my gut feeling. We did not hire him.

Was that evidence that I was more skilled at character assessments than my colleague? Absolutely not. The point of this story is to show that two people can witness the exact same interactions and walk away with two very different assessments due to personal experiences and biases. Maybe I have an unconscious negative bias toward men in blue suits. Maybe my colleague has an unconscious positive bias toward people who enjoy fishing.

My colleague and I avoided a clear mistake and eventually hired a bright young woman who excelled in the position. Our story is the same story companies can tell a thousand times over. Hiring processes are imperfect and rely on subjectivity from a limited audience. We are trusting our companies, our businesses, our livelihoods with people we have only met once or twice. Hiring is an exercise in trust. You are trusting a person to be forthcoming and honest with their background and experiences. You are trusting yourself, or the hiring manager, to assess a stranger in a very short period of time. You are trusting a stranger to enter your organization and handle information that can directly impact your business. Regardless of the level of the position, you should not take this process lightly. The stakes are high.

Always Open

One of my favorite adages for hiring is to hire the right person before you need them. How do you do this? Ensure you are **always open**. This means you are always open to hiring the right people, whether you have a job opening or not. Are you hiring? The answer is always *yes* if the right person is asking. The door is always open. Before you cringe at the cost impacts of hiring every great administrative professional, let me elaborate. Being always open is not a commitment to over-hiring. You still need to be strategic about your costs and team structure. Being always open is a mindset to being open to opportunity. When you're always open, your unsolicited applicants don't attend interviews, they have conversations.

> **Are you hiring? The answer is always yes if the right person is asking.**

I recently received a resume from a friend of a colleague. As I perused Ed's credentials, his experience aligned closely with the administrative role as a project accountant. However, we weren't hiring a new project accountant. I scoured our team to figure out if there would be any role he could fit. Questions floated around in my head. *What kind of salary does he expect? Would he fit our culture? Would his big business experience translate to our small business model?* There was no clear reason to interview him. However, conversations are free, and I am always open to a conversation. It can be a small time investment but sets no expectations and requires very little cost or effort. Instead of tossing his resume aside to save for a later date when we might have an opening, we scheduled a call with him.

In just thirty minutes, we were able to reassess his skills to fill in the details of his experience. Still, we did not have an immediate opening. It was tempting to set his resume aside to drown in the abyss of the filing cabinet. Chances are, he would not be available when our need was finally apparent, or we would forget about his resume. The stars would need to align just so, and those chances were slim. Instead of empty promises to reach out when an opportunity arose, I promised to discuss Ed's potential with the team and follow up in a week. Discussions with our team resulted in an excited flurry of suggestions for this impressive and unsolicited applicant. His potential was not an immediate fit, but was motivating enough for the leadership team to continue the conversation.

One thing that made this a great fit was that Ed's resume came to us from a referral, someone who understood our company culture and structure, and could communicate it to their friends. Ed was searching for a specific type of company through people he knew, not by simply searching job titles on a website.

By blurring the sharp edges of job requirements, your company opens opportunities to acquire talent that can take your team to the next level. If you find the right person, make the investment. They will bring value without it stemming from a prescribed job description. When you adopt the mindset of being always open, building your admin team becomes easier. You will attract talent and hone your skills for recognizing good people for your company. The best time to practice honing this skill is when the need is not pressing. I've made some of the worst hires when we're under pressure. When there is an immediate need, there is anxiety over finding someone quickly and that doesn't always lead to the best fit for the company. When you're open to applicants without that pressure, you can better assess your next A-player.

As your company builds a reputation for being a great place to work, you will begin receiving unsolicited resumes and referrals. In the context of the AM House, I invite you to start with an abundant mindset. This can be difficult for new or struggling small businesses because resources are limited. However, ideas are never limited. The idea is that you always have the tools and materials stored in your company to build a new house. Ideas are free and abundant, and the AM House is simply an idea. By realizing that new AM Houses can be built at any time, and you have everything you need to build them, the potential becomes wide and always open.

Invite Them In

Of course there will be times when the need is pressing, and you must hire someone now. Going the traditional route of job posting can be cumbersome or unyielding. If you have a general idea of the role's tasks, keep that information to the side for now. Here we will focus not on *what* they will do, but *how* they will do their administrative duties. The job *description* is a standard list of tasks they will perform. However, a job *invitation* is a quick description at the beginning of the job posting that paints the picture of your company and expectations. You're not inviting everyone; you're inviting the *right* people who will fit into your company culture.

When you draft a job invitation, focus on the culture of the company. Whether you've gone through the process of defining your mission statement and core values or not, they always exist in your company. If you have them, great. Make sure you include them in your hiring process. Even if your core values are not formalized, you can still draft an effective job invitation. Think about it as an invitation to an event. Is your company a backyard barbeque or a formal wedding?

The Backyard Barbeque

The Backyard Barbeque Company is a company where people have flexible hours. They are expected to interact informally with whomever they need to get the job done. There is a grill master cracking jokes and making sure everyone gets a full plate. At any time, you can grab a teammate for a round of corn hole or horseshoes. This type of company isn't for everyone. Your Type A neighbor with the manicured lawn may not appreciate the finger-lickin' ribs when he shows up in pressed white slacks. The Backyard Barbeque Company is laid back and fun, as long as your group doesn't get drunk and start brawling.

The Formal Wedding

The Formal Wedding Company is a company where everyone is expected to show up at a specific time, check in, and take a seat at their assigned place setting. There is a process and a schedule for everything, and everyone sticks to the program. Tables are arranged methodically with carefully selected groups of people. Everyone knows their place. When all goes according to the program, beautiful things happen. It's a gracefully orchestrated dance, as long as you don't accidentally invite the drunken grill master.

More than likely your company is somewhere in between the barbeque and wedding, but it's important to have an understanding of your company culture and express that in your job invitation. Following a cookie-cutter job posting may return a pile of resumes, but it will not help you weed through those resumes to find a good culture fit. Be upfront about your company expectations.

Give the prospective team members a feel for the company. If they are expected to show up on time and knock out tasks, tell them. If you're annoyed by people who come to you multiple times a day asking, "What's next?" be clear in the invitation. It might sound something like this:

We hire self-starters who can manage their time and responsibilities with little oversight. To thrive at our company, you must have the confidence and competence to perform tasks independently.

On the flip side, if your company embraces collaboration and you're looking for people who bring innovative ideas to the table, it might be some something like this:

We hire go-getters who are always striving to improve and enjoy exchanging feedback. To thrive at our company, you must be able to work with others and embrace change.

Craft a short invitation that works for your team and the position you're seeking. It may look slightly different for different positions but should have a common theme in the company culture. If possible, pair it with your core values. Include the brief invitation at the beginning of the job posting, followed by the requirements of the position and other pertinent information.

Just like core values, stating your expectations in the invitation once does not guarantee you'll employ the right person. It takes hearing something seven times before someone truly understands and buys into the message.[8] Restate it during the interview process and during onboarding. Ensure that you are consistently reflecting this message across meetings, gatherings, and communications.

Create Rooms with Room to Explore

Once you've invited your new admin and onboarded them into your unique company culture, there is a period of time when both you and your admin are getting to know one another. This time period can be filled with "what ifs" as you begin to trust a new person with your baby, your business. Let's explore the fears around hiring new personnel. You might be thinking:

- Did we hire the right person?
- Will they fail?
- Will we get our money's worth if they aren't productive?
- Will they mess up our carefully designed processes?
- Will I need to replace them?
- Will they get along with the team?

---

8   Keehler, John, "Marketing Frameworks To Help You Get More Patients," Forbes, Jul 6, 2021, https://www.forbes.com/sites/forbesagencycouncil/2021/07/06/marketing-frameworks-to-help-you-get-more-patients/?sh=33402f1c2d1e.

These fears are valid, but misplaced. Answering yes to the following two questions can usually alleviate any fears:

- Do they fit the culture and core values?

- Did we give them the tools they need to succeed, including time?

Once you've selected the right candidate, make good on your promises about the culture they're entering and what they can expect. Once they've stepped over the threshold and into their room, there is a balance between what the position requires and what the person brings to the position. You've set the stage for your company culture and expectations. How will you maximize their potential?

My experience with Mattesse Group is an example of the increasingly popular trend of moving away from the assembly-line mentality. You're not hiring a robot, you're hiring a whole person who has thoughts, ideas, experiences, and approaches that are inherently different from yours. There is a movement in the workplace towards authenticity and compassionate leadership, with a renewed focus on diversity of backgrounds and approaches. While a new A-player will learn your processes, they need some room to explore and bring their whole self to your team.

I've witnessed offices that are so cluttered and task-demanding that there is no room for process improvement or prioritization. Everything must be done, and it all must be done *now*. Resist the urge to bury your admin in inefficient processes and ineffective results. Without a little wiggle room, you are missing opportunities for them to make improvements and innovations that could benefit your team.

Imagine a new hire stepping over the threshold and into their AM House. The house is spacious and clean. It is open and airy. A few windows provide views to other departments and information is calmly floating in and out. Other than the windows, the walls are blank. A desk may sit in the middle or in the corner—wherever they prefer. There are no boxes or stacks of paper, maybe a filing cabinet or bookcase to hold some reference material. There is room to walk around. There is space to explore. The phone is not yet ringing, and the email is not yet pinging. They step in and take a deep breath. They've entered and it's time to get to work.

Their True Value

As you invite this new admin person into your organization, take a few extra moments to think about the way they are walking through the door, because a poor fit within your company will waste precious time and resources when it comes to managing or replacing them. Admins are especially vulnerable to poor hiring practices because the need can be urgent, qualifications can be low, and the list of tasks can be long. This trifecta of hiring rarely identifies the right person for your company and requires more management on your part after they enter their AM House. Instead, ensure you are always open for talent, then look inside the organization, and recruit based on culture as opposed to experience. Spending a few extra minutes on the front end to revise your job posting or validate candidates will save you time, money and stress on the back end. We need to cut out the dumb shit and invite the people who can elevate your team.

Once they've entered their AM House, prioritize your expectations and allow them to explore with some autonomy. You might be surprised by something they bring to the table that is unexpected and beneficial. The key to unlocking this is giving them space to explore. In the next chapter, we will discuss windows and workflows, which will help prioritize your admin's true value over the dumb shit.

⌣ Next Step

Before we move on, you can complete this simple step to get clear on the type of admin that fits with your company culture. Think about a superstar admin person that you work with now or have worked with in the past. Think of someone you wish you could clone. All costs and resources aside—if that person (or their clone) were available today, this is the person you'd hire in a heartbeat. Once you have that person clearly pictured in your head, flip to Appendix A in the back of this book or on the diagram download. In the first house diagram, write their name in the center. Under their name, write down the top three traits they possess that make them the best admin you've ever worked with. You don't have to get fancy with the wording, just write down the first 3 descriptive phrases that come to mind.

Example: Brian

- Detail oriented

- Always willing to help

- Fast learner

Next, start working your three descriptions into your hiring practices. This could be within the job posting itself or during an interview. Focus on these characteristics when you are evaluating an administrative applicant. If you don't have an applicant now, you have it recorded in Appendix A for reference. It will become part of your hiring practice in the near future.

CHAPTER 3

windows

The Bullpen

The beige fabric wall panels lining the room we called "the bullpen" did little to dampen the sound of eight people talking to each other, or on the phone. In here, no conversation was safe from lingering ears. The half-wall cubicles were more symbolic dividers than actual barriers between conversations. The room buzzed with energy: energy for the work itself, and energy for personal connections.

A large, elevated table for construction plans sprawled in the center of the room, serving less as a plans table and more as a gathering place to talk about weekend activities. There were no smoke breaks or meetings at the water cooler, but there was the plans table. Casually leaning onto the table was the equivalent of pulling up a bar stool to invite impromptu chatter.

The bullpen housed three small departments: accounting, contract administration and project management. The workflows integrated nicely because the contract admin served as the liaison between project management and accounting. As the departments interacted, it was easy to talk through the half-walls or across the plans table.

With no doors to close or conversations to muffle, I was exposed to multiple functions in the company. Within the first year I was able to overhear every project manager's conversation, ask probing questions and learn by proxy. As an email popped up with a project invoice, I hollered over to the PM, "Hey Joe, I just saw that electrical invoice you were expecting. Can I review and approve it for you?" I was able to begin to anticipate the next steps. I listened, learned, and studied.

The Move

As the company grew, we began renovating the office space. As people moved up through departments, they cycled through the bullpen, graduating from a cubicle to four solid walls. The company needed more structure and the people in the bullpen craved more private spaces for their work. The departments also grew and the bullpen could no longer house a single department, let alone three.

The framing crew came in, knocked down walls, and built new ones. Doors were installed and fresh paint replaced the fabric wall panels. Cubicles were dismantled one by one. Desks were repurposed behind closed doors. The once bustling, noisy room where people rolled their chairs a few feet out of their cubes for conversation, was quiet. The plans table loomed in its original place, vacant and lonely outside the closed doors.

The accounting department, project managers and contract admin were each moved to multiple private offices in three corners of the building—they were no longer a plans table away from a quick conversation. There was excitement and relief to have our own real offices. We brought in more family pictures to hang on walls, bought plants to fill the extra desk space, and closed our doors with a sense of importance. However, we had lost something. We became physically and informationally separated. Without the ease of proximity and conversation, we grieved the loss of comradery, and it unbridged the departments.

When we separated the departments, processes became more important. As information flowed from one department to the next, we began documenting our processes and understanding the interactions between roles. It was clear that we would need to become more structured about our workflows and more defined in our expectations of each role.

Lessons Learned

The bullpen was an exciting place to learn and grow, but it was also a bit scrappy. Roles and authority were blurred, which works well for people who are self-motivated and clear on where they want to go. I had laser focus on project management and did not get distracted (too often) by extraneous conversations. However, it was easy for anyone to get sucked into the chatter and lose track of tasks. Shared workspaces can also lead to drama and posturing as people vie for attention or recognition. We lost several people from the bullpen over the years—whether it was for lack of performance or to pursue new opportunities.

While the bullpen was open and distracting, connecting and communicating was easier. Moving to separate offices doesn't alone prevent turnover or force more efficient processes, but it does show the organization where they may be lacking. This has become increasingly relevant with the prevalence of remote work. Once each person becomes more isolated, communication deficiencies are harder to hide. For example, when the company was reconciling the finances for the month, it was easy to holler to the next cube over and ask if the project invoices were complete. Once we were separated, a formalized process was needed to keep everyone on schedule to reconcile the month. As a company we navigated this the best way we knew how—with personal conversations and collaborative effort. While we didn't consciously create clearer processes, they evolved out of necessity. As the company grew, we understood the importance of clear areas of responsibility, and we improved our processes and communication.

Windows

The story of the bullpen is quite literal. Without barriers, there is opportunity for learning and comradery. However, lack of organizational structure can create confusion and noise that interferes with the purpose of your business.

> **Whether you have an open floor plan or closed-door offices, defining the expectations for each role and building metaphorical homes will help create clarity and productivity for your team.**

Once you've brought someone through the door to their role, set them up for success within the house. Let's take a look around the metaphorical house. The windows are the openings from this house to other functions of the business. They represent the workflows and how information flows in and out of the AM House. An accounts payable window allows invoices to come in and payments to go out. An office supplies window allows supply requests to come in and a fully stocked office to go out. A website management window allows company information to come in and an updated website to go out.

I have methodically taken inventory of administrative functions and created categories of workflows. The purpose of this exercise is to identify inefficiencies and ensure the right people are performing the right tasks. While this is a worthwhile exercise, I'm not asking you to take a full and detailed inventory of your staff. I will share my lessons learned and basic rules to fast-track you through this process.

First, let's define **workflow** as it relates to windows:

A workflow is a set of steps that a person is required to do to complete a process. A workflow is a part of a larger process, and the process can involve more than one role. Therefore, when we are defining houses and windows, we want to capture the workflow that starts and stops with each role. Depending on the size of your business, your workflows can be broad or specific. The purpose of identifying workflows is to capture the most important outputs from a specific role, not to list every single task a person completes on a day-to-day basis to accomplish the output.

Through research and personal experience, a role's capacity is typically limited to no more than six workflows. When a role has more than six workflows, the priorities become muddy, the person is spread thin and it's difficult to have a handle on what they did all day. Having more than six workflows in one role is a sign that your processes are not well defined and you might be falling into the trap of the catch-all admin person. In this situation the admin person becomes the firefighter, jumping from one emergency to the next, instead of having an organized plan of attack. This isn't sustainable or scalable. If you have a person or role that you suspect has more than six workflows, I suggest you take inventory. The workflow is not the day-to-day steps to accomplish the task, it is the output of a particular role. Ask yourself, what information does this role need to pass on to the next role?

For example, at Hestel Construction the project administrators (PA) have 4 windows:

- Prime Contracts
- Subcontracts
- Invoicing
- Budgets

Let's take a closer look at the subcontracts window. The information needed to complete a subcontract comes in the window from the PM. The PA completes several individual steps inside their room, and at the end of the workflow, a fully executed subcontract and all of its associated requirements goes out the window to the superintendent. This single window has a specific purpose that is part of a larger pre-construction process. The output is proof to the superintendent that a subcontractor is qualified and approved to proceed with the work.

Window Varieties

The information that flows in and out of the windows in your business is going to be unique. However, there are a few basic windows that exist in almost all businesses:

- Accounts Payable (A/P)

- Accounts Receivable (A/R)
- Payroll
- Sales
- Marketing
- Operations
- Business Administration (licensing, insurance, taxes, registrations, etc.)

Each of these windows can be divided into associated administrative windows. If you're struggling to identify windows, start with this list and expand or divide the categories to customize it to your structure.

A smaller business may have a single person filling multiple roles with broad windows. For example, in a very small business, your sales manager might also be your bookkeeper, who might also be your marketer. In this case, a single person can occupy a house with multiple rooms but you should still limit this person's capacity to six windows.

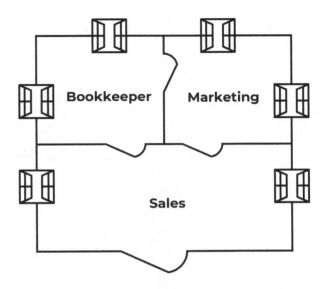

Why not place all six, unrelated windows in the same room? It's important to keep the roles separated. As you grow, having distinct roles will make it easier to add people to your team, setting everyone up for success. Separating the roles into rooms makes it easier to break off a role for a new AM House as the company grows. If one person is doing it all, with no clarity on the multiple roles they are filling, tension will build as new staff come on board.

As businesses grow, each team member's focus becomes narrower and volume increases. It's perfectly acceptable to have fewer than six windows if the volume is high. For example, in a high-volume accounting department, one person may be dedicated to accounts payable. In this case, the workflows may be separated by payment type, for instance, which may be fewer than six.

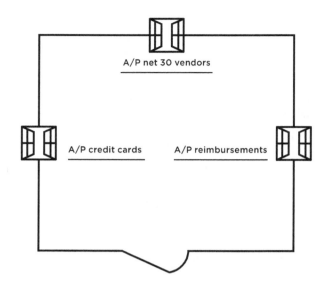

A/P net 30 vendors

A/P credit cards   A/P reimbursements

Rooms without Windows

Should there ever be a house with no windows? Let's think about that for a minute. A house without windows would be a position with no output, no results, no means to measure if someone is doing their job well. Someone who may organize and file other people's information, without really *doing* anything with it, could be an example of a room with no windows. When I was sixteen, I had a part-time job at a car dealership that paid five dollars and twenty-five cents an hour. I was placed in a cubicle in the room above the showroom to put papers in alphabetical order. For hours. This position was entirely made-up because I was a family friend. I would argue this position had no windows, or just maybe one of those half-windows near the top of the wall that are found in basements.

Do you know what a house with no windows reminds me of? Outhouses. People who are hired to do dumb shit are metaphorically working in bathrooms.... with all that shit. For goodness sake, if you have anyone working in a house without windows, give them some circulation and open a window.

Engineer Your Windows

I have worked with business coach, Walt Brown, across multiple companies for years. He taught us to perform an exercise in defining roles in each of the companies, he lovingly called *flower power*. Having performed this exercise with dozens of unique roles, I've witnessed the benefits and must give credit where credit is due. I provide the abridged version here, but you can read the full scope of his teachings in his book *Death of the Org Chart*.

Before you engineer your team, try this exercise with yourself first. Write your name or your position in the middle of a square. Take inventory of everything you do in a typical workday. What workflows are you an integral part of? What results are you accountable for? Try to get more specific than "run the business" or "the bottom line." If you are the director of operations, your list might look something like this:

- Hire & fire staff
- Run production meetings

- Meet with key customers
- Quality control
- Schedule staff
- Train staff
- Budget
- Negotiate
- Long-term strategy
- Analyze production data
- Troubleshoot
- Process & procedure documentation
- Identify production efficiencies/inefficiencies
- Address customer concerns

You can then categorize this list into larger workflows. For example, hire & fire staff, run production meetings, schedule staff and train staff are all related to, you guessed it, staff. Staffing is one of your windows. You can get more specific and call it production staffing or operations staffing, but you get the gist. You might get insight or input from others on your team, but you ultimately have a responsibility around staffing your team.

Go down the list and create other categories that can be your windows. Visualize yourself in a house with a few open windows. Imagine information floating, or *flying*, into a window. You analyze it, test it, change it, document it, process it, collaborate on it, and eventually, send it back out through the window with an action or decision. It might not be the final decision or action, but you've done your part and it goes to the next step in the larger process. After you've taken the time to engineer your room, it's time to move on. While it's helpful to understand your role, this exercise was meant to get you into the right frame of mind to analyze your admin team.

The goal is to map out the tasks for each of your admin people and categorize them into six or fewer windows. You might be tempted to jump straight to creating their windows. You might think, "I know what Tom does. I hired him." However, when you're constructing your admin's house, it's a worthwhile exercise to make a list of all tasks for each of your admin people. I'm willing to bet they are engaging in tasks that you didn't realize. That doesn't make you a bad boss but asking the questions will help you to become a better boss.

> **The questions and discussions that arise from doing a deep dive into your admin staff's tasks will create clarity for them, you, and the team.**

Importance of Clarity

The importance of getting clarity around your processes and workflows is assumed, but widely disregarded, by the new small business owner when it comes to administration. Hiring that catch-all admin person seems simple at first. They will answer emails, track some basic information, and assist you when needed. But first and foremost, make sure your admin has windows and isn't trapped in the basement or outhouse. Both you and your admin need to understand that they have valuable output and define what that output looks like. Everyone needs to have a deliverable or metric for which they are accountable.

As your business grows, existing windows will get larger and new windows will appear. Don't lose track of your admin;s capacity for six windows. A periodic evaluation of processes and windows will ensure your processes stay current and efficient, and your admin aren't spread too thin. Whether it's changing a process to eliminate an inefficient workflow, automating processes to reduce workflows, redistributing workflows to spread the workload, or hiring a new admin, find the solution that works for your team to keep the capacity at six or fewer windows. It's an anchoring rule that will reduce burnout and keep space open for new ideas.

So far, we have invited your admin through the front door and explored their six windows. These two elements address *who* and *what* travels through the house without constructing the outer shell of the house. It's important to understand for whom you're building the house and what it will accommodate before you frame the walls. To complete the shell of the house, we need to define the outer limits of our walls and roof. Now that you have a good handle on your admin's day-to-day responsibilities, we'll bring additional clarity to their role by defining titles and purpose statements that will anchor the location and define the walls of the AM House.

🪟 Next Step

You may not have the time to take inventory of every workflow for your admin team, but take a few minutes to do a gut check. Think of your admin from the last exercise, the name written in the house in Appendix A. Does your gut tell you that they are spread too thin? Even if they are incredibly organized, do they put in long hours or skip lunch because they have too much to do?

If the answer is *no*, congratulations! Your admin is in the minority for small businesses and your assignment is easy. Take a moment today or tomorrow to thank your admin for their support and ask them to write down their six most important workflows. If this feels awkward, share with them that you are reading a book about helping your team clarify their roles and would love their help. People are receptive to helping in this way if they understand where your request is coming from. And this type of exercise is right up the admin's alley.

If the answer is *yes*, don't fret. Most small business admins are spread too thin. Still, take a moment today or tomorrow to thank your admin for their support. Then, mark a date on your calendar when you can sit down with your admin for thirty minutes to list the workflows they cover. If your admin is spread thin, do not ask them to do this exercise alone. Your participation is critical to help organize their thoughts and differentiate tasks from workflows. There might be some processes, workflows or tasks that jump out right away as an issue that has a quick solution. I've frequently had these types of discussions where I've discovered that someone was performing a task that was outdated, unnecessary, or miscommunicated. You won't solve all the issues of a spread-thin admin in thirty minutes, but it will weed out the obvious inefficiencies and create a baseline for future decisions.

Whether your admin was able to write down their six workflows or you compiled the list together, flip to Appendix A and label your AM House's six windows. You are just starting to build your first AM House—resist the urge to skip ahead until you've read through the next eight chapters.

CHAPTER 4

address

Taking a Risk

Snacks, cups, unopened mail and kids' crafts cluttered every surface of the kitchen. It was a typical Saturday evening at Laura's house with the kids playing in the basement, husbands in the living room, and three good friends chatting in the kitchen. Laura, Terry and I leaned against the cream-colored island with a bottle of wine in the center and glasses in hand.

"I love my new job," Terry boasted about a construction company she'd recently joined. "They're only a few years old, but they've grown from a two-million-dollar to a ten-million-dollar company in the past couple of years. The owner, Darrell, is brilliant."

My ears perked up. At this point I was well established in my role as a project manager and starting to dabble in business development. I hadn't considered leaving my job, but my head swirled with the possibilities of joining a fresh new company. I flung questions at Terry about the company's capabilities and potential.

My head was full of what-ifs, and I decided that the first step, a very low-risk step, was to draft a letter. I could write a letter. I didn't have to send it. I drafted a propositional cover letter that highlighted my experience in construction management and business development. I offered a skill set that this small company lacked, and I promised to deliver growth for the company. It wasn't that I was unhappy with my current position, it was simply an exercise in risk and reward. Maybe they would throw the letter in the trash. Maybe they wouldn't.

With the letter drafted, I could take the next tiny step—which was still low risk—and send it to my friend. I didn't need to send it directly to the company. Then, it would be out of my hands. Maybe she would throw it in the trash. Maybe she would pass it on.

She passed it on. The letter was confident and appealing, landing me an immediate invitation to interview.

The Great Title Debate

The company was structured like any typical, small, family-owned construction firm. It had an all-male labor force, female administrators, and a few technical specialists. The only woman in leadership was the owner's wife, who was the CFO. From the outside looking in, the company operated well, and its employees seemed happy.

The interview had gone exceptionally well, and I was both excited and nervous to take on the new position. When the owner called me after the interview, he was equally excited to make an offer. I had not applied for any specific role but wanted to take the next step in operations management. The exact title and responsibilities were undefined. From my viewpoint, this was an excellent opportunity to create my perfect job for growth.

The owner expressed his excitement to bring me on board because he desired another person in leadership. I expressly stated how I could grow the company through my experience working with other larger contractors and federal customers. We spoke on the phone several times over the course of two weeks, trying to define the position.

"I'm thinking *director of administration*," he proposed. My heart sank. There was the A-word: *administration*. After selling myself hard in business development and project management, he put me right back in my place as *administrative*. I ignored my gut and steered the conversation back to my objective: to grow as a female leader in operations in a male-dominated industry.

"I'd rather stay away from defining it as *administration*. I currently work in operations and that's what I enjoy. I think I can serve the company better by focusing on operations and business development." I rebutted.

He hesitated and mildly scoffed at my sensitivity to the A-word, but we finally settled on *program manager*. I continued to view it as an opportunity to build on my strengths and define my role in a way that motivated me and benefited the company. Before officially accepting the position, I requested to meet with the team for a casual meet and greet. The company culture was important because I subscribe to the notion that *who* you work with is more important than *what* you do. Darrell gladly invited me to a luncheon at their office.

What Does Autonomy Mean?

"I think Darrell is smitten with you," my friend said to me over the phone. Darrell wanted me to join the team and was putting forth extra effort to recruit me. This was a small company, not a Fortune 500 where they wine and dine their leadership recruits. Even this modest luncheon was a rare luxury for their hiring process. I was flattered by the gesture.

As we sat around the table with our deli sandwiches on paper plates and solo cups filled with iced tea, we shared our professional backgrounds and engaged in small talk about our families and where we grew up. Darrell was the only man at the table. The president was absent. The small conference table held five women in addition to me: his wife, the CFO; my friend, the HR manager; the bookkeeper; the admin assistant; and the marketing associate. Other than Darrell, there wasn't a single person at the table who worked in operations. They were all intelligent people who worked hard and seemed to enjoy their jobs. Other than Darrell and his wife, none of the attendees had a background in business or construction. Darrell was demonstrating his ability to hire from entry-level and train up.

Darrell steered the conversation back to the potential of my joining the team. "Do you have any questions for them?" he asked, gesturing to the other members at the table.

"Absolutely. I'd love to hear more about the management style here. Is everyone given the space and trust to work autonomously?" I admit, it was a leading question where I had a clear expectation for them to respond in the affirmative. I did not anticipate the response I received.

Darrell and his wife eyed the team. I watched in bewilderment as the team exchanged glances with each other. After a few uncomfortable moments of silence, Megan the marketer spoke up, "What does that mean? Autonomously?"

When no one answered, Darrell jumped in "Do you know what autonomous means?" he asked his team. Megan, again, gave an uncomfortable response with a slow shake of her head.

I can't recall the rest of the luncheon because my brain was stuck. These intelligent adults did not understand the concept of autonomy in the workplace. I convinced myself that it was just a word. They must have understood the concept of being able to manage your own time and responsibilities. I had thrown them off with my choice of words. It wasn't them; it was me. After all, my friend loved working there. Surely she worked autonomously.

What's the Purpose?

I ignored the red flags, and took the job. I was inundated with various administrative tasks—and truthfully, I was overwhelmed with the lack of sophistication in their general processes—but I tackled them because I wanted to prove my value. I knew how to develop processes. I knew how to make workflows more efficient. But that was not my expectation of this position. I asked many times within those first two weeks about the purpose of my position as program manager. What programs was I expected to manage? Darrell's response was, "Your job is to manage me."

Shortly after that I called my previous boss and asked if the position I left was still available. Not only was my previous boss accepting, he was ecstatic to welcome me back to the team as if I'd never left. On the third Friday—less than one month since I'd started with the new company—I requested a meeting with Darrell. I sat across from his desk once again nervous and excited for a change.

"I don't think this will come as a surprise to you," I started, "This is not working, and I've accepted an offer to return to my previous company. I am turning in my two weeks' notice effective today." I was right. He was not surprised.

"You can leave now," was his only response. As scary as it was to sit across from him and receive the abrupt termination, I let out an internal breath of relief. This was the last day, last hour, last minute I had to endure this uncomfortable relationship.

I was ready to return to a company who appreciated me, challenged me and encouraged me to explore my own purpose.

Lessons Learned

This is an extreme example of misaligning with management style, but it's moreso an example of a poorly defined title and purpose. I ignored the signs and dove into the new adventure with blind optimism.

When I reflect on my very short experience at Darrell's company, my initial reaction is anger and frustration that I allowed Darrell to make me feel unworthy of a leadership position at his company. It is easy to point the finger at him as an authoritarian leader. However, I can point to a few things that Darrell did well during the hiring process that convinced me to join his team:

- He was open to hiring someone for talent and not for a directly identified position.
- He allowed input in developing my title.
- He gave me space to explore the company.

So where did it go sideways? I should have paid more attention to the title he initially suggested. It clearly delineated his expectation of my purpose. A director of administration is not expected to run operations or seek growth opportunities, the things that I was interested in doing. A director of administration's purpose is to improve and implement administrative processes. If I had asked more questions around his suggestion of my title, rather than pushing my agenda, I might have saved us all some time—and certainly saved my tears. The director of administration is a very respectable title and was a better fit for Darrell's expectations of the purpose of the position.

What's in a Title?

There is a reason I waited until this far into the book to introduce titles. It may seem like the first decision we make when we need to hire someone, "We need an admin assistant." However, if you take the time to contemplate a role's primary windows and the requirements before entering the house, you're in a much better position to contemplate a title and purpose that will set up this new role for success.

As millennials begin to make up a larger portion of our workforce, it's important to remember that they are more likely to move from one job to the next and to look for opportunities for growth. Millennials are resume builders and titles are important on resumes.

Common titles make it easier for Search Engine Optimization (SEO) to attract resumes but do little to help a new hire understand their purpose. What is the purpose of an admin assistant? To assist the administrators? To assist with the administration of what? What does that even mean? What does it look like? In the hit TV series, *The Office*, Dwight Schrute is the assistant to the regional manager. However, he often squabbles with his boss, Michael Scott, as he frequently tries to call himself the assistant regional manager. Why? Because no one wants to be known as someone's assistant. Assisting the person implies a "lesser than" status.

Think about the exercise outlined in chapter three around engineering the windows. The title for a role should directly relate to the primary window or collection of windows that belongs to each house. If the person's primary windows are all related to receiving, processing, and completing the paperwork related to new orders, they might be a sales coordinator or an order specialist or a processing agent or purchase order administrator.

Get creative. Get input.
Stay away from generic assistant titles.

Purpose

Do you wake up energized to lead your team, or dreading all the little things that need to get done? Every one of your employees needs a reason to get out of bed and go to work in the morning besides money. So do you. Elevating the purpose for your team will in turn elevate yours. Everyone at your company has a job, but how many understand their purpose? Even your entry-level people have a purpose. Your job is to help them discover it. A purpose statement is not a five-paragraph essay. It should be one or two sentences that give someone clarity on their contribution to the bigger picture.

Her job is to manage me is a bullshit purpose statement. You're an adult. Your job is to manage yourself. Her job might be to manage your calendar, but her purpose is to ensure that everyone who needs a piece of your day is scheduled accordingly. In this way, she is serving your customers (or vendors, employees, service providers, etc.) not you. However, my guess is that your admin staff do a whole lot more than manage your calendar. In fact, they probably do more than you realize because they make your job easier. But that does not give you the liberty to cop out of understanding their roles. You're the boss and your job is to understand your people.

A wise woman once reflected on her earlier career as an admin assistant and told me, "Other people in the organization don't realize what an admin does because part of her job is to put out fires before they make it to the rest of the team. That's part of the conundrum—if the admin is good at her job, then no one else ever knows how much she does until she's not there."

My advice to you is to spend a little more time understanding what your admins do, not just their daily tasks, but their most valuable contributions. Those contributions may be the fires that go unnoticed.

Address – The Importance of Defining Roles

As much as owners and managers should understand their admin roles, their team should also understand how their roles contribute to the success of the company. Houses need strong walls to withstand storms. In your AM House, we want directional identifiers to withstand organizational fluctuations. Defining the role with a clear title and purpose statement does just that. It is the address. It's the outward message to the rest of the company, customers and vendors that tell them what information belongs in this house and which problems this house can solve. The clearer the message, the stronger the walls.

You must avoid paper walls, or walls without any structural support behind them. Using a generic title with no definitive purpose builds weak walls that can be torn down easily by a few gusts of wind, or demanding colleagues. Let's take our ubiquitous admin assistant, for example. No one in the organization knows exactly what they do, but they are always there to help with odds and ends. But all it takes is one messy manager to start breaking down the walls. The messy manager continually leans on the admin assistant as a personal assistant, making their purpose fuzzy and the windows unsecure. At that point, any one tumultuous event will blow the whole house down, leaving a pile of rubble and costing the company time and resources to clean it up.

Helping administrative staff understand their purpose is a gift. It gives them the authority and a way to prioritize their work. Let's explore Destiny's story as an example. Destiny is the primary bookkeeper and payroll processor at her company. She developed her purpose statement:

My purpose is to make sure that everyone gets paid accurately in a timely manner—the company, our vendors, and our employees.

This purpose statement drives her to follow up on her receivable collections to keep the aging list to a minimum; to pay her vendors on time so they continue to deliver; and to take care of the employees by ensuring their paychecks are correct. This is crystal clear to anyone else in the company who may lean on her for tasks outside her purpose. When Bill, a remote sales manager, calls to ask Destiny for help troubleshooting his computer, it's clearly not a part of her purpose statement.

What would be the harm in Destiny taking five minutes to help Bill? I've seen this happen countless times and have done it myself, trying to be the helpful admin. This is the type of task that sounds easy enough but often develops into something far more time consuming than expected. This just leads to the admin now taking responsibility to resolve something that's outside of the role's purpose.

Eventually, Destiny could help Bill reconnect his computer to the company's server and save the day. Bill will not remember what Destiny did or said to fix his computer, but he will remember that he was frustrated, and Destiny fixed it. And what will happen when Bill gets frustrated next time? Bill will call Destiny again and it will snowball because Bill isn't the only one who gets frustrated with administrative tools. Destiny's purpose will become unstable and eventually, Destiny will be the one who is frustrated.

However, what if Destiny has the clear authority to stick to her purpose? In this case, her response might be, "Bill, it sounds like you need some help with your computer. Got it. However, my number one priority today is payroll, and I need to make sure you get paid. I don't have time to fix your computer right now, but I'll teach you how to log an IT help request, and they will get back to you within an hour."

Destiny didn't brush off Bill or tell him outright that she was too busy. She was still the helpful admin but leaned on her purpose to prioritize her response. Furthermore, she taught Bill how to log an IT request so that he is more likely to do this next time, instead of calling Destiny for computer help. Bill has a new tool to resolve his frustration and Destiny stays within her purpose. Bill gets back to work, and Destiny's house stands strong.

Traps

Having a clear title and purpose is empowering for your admins. When the title and purpose are defined with intention and are in alignment with the company's vision and priorities, it solidifies the admin's role and moves the whole company forward.

Misaligned Purpose

The first common trap in this is the misaligned purpose. This can happen when admins create their own title or assume their purpose without your buy-in. Admins may think they understand your priorities, but I've seen many misinterpretations happen. The perfect example is my experience with Darrell. He gave me the space to create my title and purpose, but it was misaligned with his needs.

Familiar Purpose

The second trap is the familiar purpose. An admin who has vast experience in one area will attempt to relate their past purpose with the new purpose that you need. When they are hired for a specific responsibility that is related, but not exactly the same as their past experience, they may fall back on their previous experience out of comfort and familiarity. This stunts their growth and violates the new purpose. While the admin may think they are performing well, it's only compared to the past, familiar purpose. This leads to frustrated bosses.

Shifting Purpose

The third common trap is the shifting purpose. The admin thinks their purpose is A. One day the boss walks in and says, "I need you to work on B. It's important." Without further clarification, the admin shifts their priority and purpose from A to B. After all, the boss said B was important. The next week, the boss wonders why the admin isn't focused on A.

This leads to frustrated admin staff and inefficiencies associated with shifting priorities. Unfortunately, bosses will do this out of necessity and not realize how their admin interprets the instruction.

So how do we avoid these traps? The most important rule is to not develop purpose statements in a vacuum. Both you and your admin person should have input and ultimately agree on the purpose statement. Next, make that statement clear and usable. Whether it's a poster on their wall or a simple sticky note, the admin should refer to it often so they can compare new requests against it for alignment. Finally, empower your admin to raise the question when something doesn't align. This is where trust and relationships are important. When you and your admin have a trusting and open relationship, the admin will feel comfortable enough to question your intentions. Some bosses are perfectly comfortable with an admin who asks WTF? Others prefer a more conservative approach.

Creating Space and Planting Gardens

By developing a short purpose statement for your admin, it gives them space to explore new ways to work that stay in alignment with their purpose. There should always be some core processes to follow, but they should not be so rigid that they stifle new ideas that might make the company more efficient or effective. With Destiny's purpose statement as an example, she can explore new integrated accounting or payroll software, find ways to compile employee time cards, or automate recurring payments. She might also find ways to make the company more enjoyable by automating beautiful "thank you" emails that are sent when the company receives payment from a customer.

It's important to allow your admin some space to breathe and opportunities to bring their own ideas to the table. While the purpose should be clear and concise, it does not serve as handcuffs. It is a tool for people outside the house, looking in. It ensures they know exactly why the house stands and it keeps the occupant focused on the priorities of the company.

Ideally the admin is bringing new ideas that fit within the limits of the house. Occasionally you will find an admin who has talents and interests that benefit the company beyond their primary purpose. If your admin's house has a clear title and purpose statement with strong walls, they might find enjoyment in and be passionate about something unrelated to their primary purpose. It isn't necessary to find room in their house for these duties. If the primary purpose of their role is their house, their additional talent for auxiliary duties is their garden.

Gardens can be beautiful additions to a house, bringing additional growth, color and oxygen to its owner. Gardens can come in the form of charities, social gatherings, involvement in associations, music, art, recycling, and so on. It's a passion that creeps into the company without an expressed need, but enhances it nonetheless. It's something that gives the admin's house a personal touch and grows unique talents. It isn't a required talent or skill or responsibility. It is purely chosen and nurtured by the admin. It is sometimes abandoned by the admin, without recourse.

Jennifer is an assistant who takes her job seriously and keeps the inside of her house in order, always meeting deadlines and keeping project files organized. She became involved with an industry association a few years back and has been attending workshops to develop her career and skills. The association has been mutually beneficial for the company and thus, the company supports her involvement. This year, she volunteers to organize an industry event to raise money for a charity to support underprivileged children during the Christmas holiday. As a child who once benefited from this type of charity, Jennifer is passionate about the project. She wants it to be a huge success and records every detail so that it is repeatable in future seasons. With the blessing of her boss, she spends two hours a week organizing the event for eight weeks leading up to the event. During this time, she continues to meet her primary responsibilities inside her AM House.

This charity event is Jennifer's garden. She nurtures it for eight weeks a year. It helps develop her planning, marketing, and management skills as she coordinates vendors and develops relationships with other businesses who participate. The ability to give back to the community brings her joy and satisfaction beyond her personal career goals.

Your job in the garden is to encourage and admire the garden, but not require the plants to grow. Remember that the garden is a bonus. In Jennifer's example, she could decide not to run the event next year. While this might be disappointing to the association and beneficiaries, she should not face any recourse in her primary position at the company. Any position requirement belongs inside the house. Conversely, she has the approval of her boss to dedicate some time to the event project, and she must keep a pulse on whether it is detracting from her primary responsibilities. The admin's job is to keep the house standing strong before planting anything in the garden because a beautiful garden can be easily crushed by a collapsing house.

A Signal for What Belongs

The title and purpose of your admin's house is the outer shell that signals to the rest of the organization, customers and vendors, exactly what belongs in this house. The exterior wall displays the address, which is a map to administrative information. The title and purpose should be both outwardly clarifying and inwardly strengthening. It gives others clarity on the admin's roles and responsibilities. It gives the admin clarity on their priorities and the authority to redirect requests that distract them from those priorities. The important step is to make sure you are clear and aligned with the admin's purpose. Misaligned or shifting purpose statements lead to frustrated admin staff and bosses. Be aware of the purpose traps: misaligned purpose, familiar purpose, and shifting purpose. A clear purpose includes the expectations of the boss *and* the focus of the admin.

The beautiful part of the exterior of the AM House is the garden. If your admin brings their outside talents and passions to enhance your company or their experience, nurture those gardens. Gardens make for happy and motivated people. A motivated admin with a clear and aligned purpose sets them up for success in our next chapter: ownership.

> **The important step is to make sure you are clear and aligned with the admin's purpose. Misaligned or shifting purpose statements lead to frustrated admin staff and bosses.**

 Next Step

Step 1

Use the window exercise that you completed at the end of chapter three. Whether your rockstar admin listed their own or it took a joint effort, refer to Appendix A's labeled windows. Next, ask yourself these questions:

- Does the title accurately reflect these windows?
- Is there a clarifying theme around the windows?

Above the house in Appendix A, write your admin's current title in the address box. If the title is directly related to the windows and accurately signals to the outside world the purpose of your admin's role, leave the title as it is. If their title is generic or doesn't accurately relate to their primary workflows, highlight or otherwise mark the title in a way that will remind you to revisit this with your admin during their next performance review. Unless your admin is drowning and needs a change now, I recommend waiting until your natural review cycle to make a title change.

Step 2

Next is the purpose statement. This is a much trickier exercise because it must be aligned with the company's vision and the admin's interpretation of their priorities. At the performance review, take a stab at creating a purpose statement together. You can share sections of this chapter with them prior to the review to help prepare them to discuss their purpose statement. A purpose statement includes the priority of the admin as it relates to the company.

The following are examples of purpose statements for a few standard administrative roles:

- A payroll and bookkeeping admin's purpose is to ensure everyone is paid correctly in a timely manner.

- An executive assistant's purpose is to make sure the boss' time is scheduled and communicated in order of priority.

- An office manager's purpose is to make sure the facility is always stocked and serviced.

- A human resource manager's job is to enforce legal and company policies while protecting employee compensation, benefits and rights.

You can use these purpose statements as a starting point or simply as a reference when creating them for your own team. Get creative with these statements so that you and your team are fully aligned. Bookmark this page and set a reminder on your calendar to reference it before the next performance review with your admin team. There is a place to write the purpose statement in the house in Appendix A, and you can write one now or come back to it after the performance review. If you write one now, do not become too attached. Remember the traps of misaligned, familiar, and shifting purpose statements. Appendix A is simply practice until you have the time to consult with your admin.

CHAPTER 5

the deed

No-show

Sonya came into my office, sighed and slumped into the chair across from my desk. "Mindy is a no-show again today. I had to send Lisa to fill in for her. Lisa is a team player, but we can't keep doing this. I need Lisa back with the accounting team. This sucks, I really like Mindy." Having counseled Mindy in the past about her attendance and lack of communication, it was time to let her go.

Mindy's position was a struggle to fill. It was a traditional receptionist position which required very little experience. The only real requirements were reliability, a good attitude, and the ability to learn some basic administrative tasks. We tacked on some auxiliary tasks to fill the eight-hour day, but still did not require any credentials. It should be the easiest to fill because almost anyone qualified. At first, our theory proved true and we received a flood of resumes.

We sent several follow-up emails and made many phone calls to applicants, but they went unanswered. The few who responded and set up interviews pulled no-shows themselves. Lisa continued to be the team player who covered the front desk and incoming phone calls while performing her accounting responsibilities. Sonya appreciated her willingness to help, but she was missing opportunities to grow in her primary role.

After weeks of searching and failed attempts to interview, Sonya was excited to finally have a responsive applicant. Our new receptionist arrived on time the first day with a complacent smile. We didn't read much into her complacency because we were so relieved to have someone in the chair. She was perfectly capable of doing the job. However, it wasn't long before we started having the same issues as Mindy. She stopped showing up on time and occasionally didn't show up at all. The cycle started over again with unresponsive applicants. We tried a temporary placement agency, but the entry-level people that they sent to us also moved on. Six months went by as we cycled through receptionists without finding a permanent placement.

What's missing?

Back in the same chair across from my desk—once again dealing with an uncommitted receptionist—Sonya's frustration was palpable. "Why can't we find any responsible people? It shouldn't be this hard to find someone who can just show up when they're supposed to!" Sonya gestured with her hands on either side of her head, as if it were about to explode. She was spending time and resources filling a position she thought should be easy. What was going wrong?

We sat down together to brainstorm. We needed a reliable person to answer phones and perform some basic tasks. This seemed like a common position in businesses; doesn't every brick and mortar business have a receptionist? What were we missing? I reflected on my own experience as a receptionist, the result of a placement through an employment agency. I was only in the seat for a few weeks to fill in while the permanent receptionist was recovering from surgery. The permanent receptionist at that company was loyal and dependable. She was an older woman who had been there for many years and had an air of seniority about her. Even though her title was *receptionist*, she had implied authority earned through her tenure and the close relationship she developed with the owner of the company. The receptionist didn't make decisions for the company, but everyone knew she had the owner's ear. That kind of confidence would be impossible to find in a new person as it only would come with tenure.

Options

"We need to pay a little more, but just throwing money at it won't fix the problem." I suggested. "We need to change the position. What do we really want? Do we really want someone who just answers phones?"

We continued to brainstorm ways to expand the position. We could automate our phones and get rid of the position all together *or* we could elevate that position to attract more qualified people. We were a growing company who wanted more talented people who could grow with us. We increased the salary, increased the required experience, and increased the responsibility.

Adding responsibility to the job wasn't just about lengthening the list of duties. It required a deeper dive into company processes to determine which tasks belonged with a new position. Since the receptionist was the conduit for communication coming into the company, it made sense for them to be a conduit of information within the organization as well. Managing email blasts and contacts lists fit nicely into the job description. While the receptionist was responsible for opening and routing mail, it also made sense that they could document and track the insurance updates that frequently arrived in hard copy. As we continued to make these connections, the description evolved into a multidimensional role that attracted experienced administrators.

We were still flooded with resumes—some relevant and others not. Of the applicants that we contacted, the response rate increased significantly, and they showed up for the interview. Instead of grasping at the only responsive applicant, we finally had options—including professional administrators with experience doing more than just showing up on time.

Lessons Learned

On the surface, our solution to the receptionist problem seems simple: offer more money, require more experience, get better people. However, the root of the problem is a larger issue that is prevalent among administrative staff. At first glance it seems that inexperienced people are unreliable. If this were truly the problem, throwing money and requiring experience would fix it. However, without increasing the authority of the position, we would still suffer high turnover. The root of the problem wasn't money or experience. The root of the problem was not enabling the position to have authority over their area of responsibility. Answering phones and performing tasks as prescribed by other people gives the receptionist little control over their own day. This leads to boredom, a lack of motivation, and neglect.

Why would someone be motivated to excel if their primary responsibility was to show up? "That's what we pay you for," is a common answer. Sorry, boss, but paying someone minimum wage isn't intrinsically motivating. I'd rather work at the fast-food joint down the street because I'd have more authority at the drive-through than I would answering your phones. The sixteen-year-old at the cash register is trusted with more authority than our twenty-five-year-old receptionist routing phone calls.

Trust vs. Micromanagement

By immediately signaling respect and giving someone authority in their area of responsibility, leaders pave the way for employee loyalty, retention, growth, and productivity. The most important part of employee retention and satisfaction relates to feeling valued and being engaged. According to the Gallup Paper *Re-engineering Performance Management*, "Employees are demanding a shift away from traditional performance management practices and toward 'performance development' that is individualized to their natural talents, performance needs and sense of purpose."[9] Feeling valued and engaged is more than a quick thank you, or the classic annual review. It is instilling trust in your team, giving them the authority to make decisions about their own processes, allowing flexibility in the structure of their workday, and recognizing innovation.

"But they have to earn my respect and trust," some owners argue. After all, an owner is trusting a team with their personal creation and assets. Many owners do not withhold trust out of maniacal control or calculated strategy, **they withhold it out of fear**. I get it—you're trusting your company with people

---

9   Wigert, Ben and Harter, Jim, "Re-engineering Performance Management," Gallup, Inc., 2017, https://www.gallup.com/workplace/238064/re-engineering-performance-management.aspx.

who aren't as invested as you and that's scary. Your investment, assets, home, credit rating, and reputation are on the line.

> You've sacrificed your time with your family and all things valuable to build a great company. No one will ever take it as seriously as you do.

Owners who struggle with letting go of the reins get caught in the weeds of every detail to make sure it doesn't fail. They spend time fixing the small things because they feel just as impactful as the big things. *How could you possibly trust a lower-level admin to care for your company the way you would?* This sense of protection not only prevents owners from working on the strategies and vision for which they started the company in the first place, it prevents their team from stepping up and owning their contributions to the company.

There are only two reasons for micromanaging your team. It's either them or it's you. If you are spending too much time fixing their mistakes, reiterating processes, and coaching through basic decisions, reevaluate who you have in the seats. Sometimes it just takes the right person to grab hold of a position and run with it. If your employees have the ability and desire to take hold of their processes and run with them, your job is to pave the way for their sprint and help them when they trip.

However, if you are spending your time or resources correcting mistakes that don't impact the overall process because you're chasing perfection, the problem might be you. Some managers enjoy getting caught in the weeds because it creates small wins. Aha! You've found a report that's missing five dollars in interest. Fixing that is less daunting than generating an additional $500,000 in revenue to meet your quarterly goals. If you're spending your time on the small stuff to avoid the big stuff, *pause*, put this book down, do some self-reflection, get your priorities straight, then come back and reread this book.

Micromanaging an admin team is easy to do because there are many repetitive tasks and multiple ways to accomplish them. While there might only be a couple ways to sweep a floor, there are many ways to organize employee files or generate invoices. It's easy to have an opinion on how it's being done. Micromanagers have a hard time lifting themselves out of the "how" and to focus on the "what" or "why." *What* needs to be done? The employee files need to be organized. *Why* does it need to be done? The information must be easy to locate for anyone who needs to access them. *How* they are organized is a function that should be up to the admin person. The trap for micromanagers is when they attempt to step back and let their employee figure out a project, then nit-pick the results. If you find yourself doing any of the following, you might be a micromanager:

- Becoming frustrated or taking over because you can do the task faster/better.

- Criticizing the outcome without questioning your original direction.
- Re-doing tasks that were delegated to your team.
- Spending just as much time on a project as the person you assigned to it.

The key to battling micromanagement is clearly painting the picture of the outcome you expect, then allowing your team to figure out how to get there—offering an open door to answer questions and provide clarifications along the way.

Don't be a Hoarder

Everyone knows a hoarder. They keep every little knick-knack that carries an ounce of sentimental value. They are afraid to throw out, sell, or give anything away. Their garages, attics, and living rooms are full of stuff that might have been valuable at one time but is t taking up space. They feel that everything has value and one day they might need that thing they've been storing for five years. The collection of stuff makes it difficult to move around and it gets in the way of the important functions of the home. When was the last time you saw an episode of *Hoarders* in a big beautiful, well-maintained home? You won't because the hoarder cannot clean or maintain the home with all that junk in the way. In extreme examples it negatively impacts the people who are attempting to support the hoarder. You also won't see an episode where the family of the hoarder is happy and supportive. The typical episode portrays a frustrated and sad family member at the end of their rope.

Don't be a business hoarder. If you're hoarding ownership of all responsibilities in your business, it will undoubtedly have a negative impact on your productivity and your team's. Hoarding ownership keeps your team at arm's length by treating them as renters, preventing them from investing their time and effort in your company. It will wear you down and cause high turnover as you try to "control the renters." Hoarding ownership limits your potential for growth because your team will never have the opportunity to improve processes they can't own. It will get in the way of your most critical functions, take up your time, and undermine the structure of your company. At worst, hoarding ownership threatens the structure of *your* leadership house. The cost of hoarding the knick-knacks is huge. Think about your goals and vision. Whether your leadership house is built to grow the business, or so that you can spend more time with your family, you can't possibly clear your house for its bigger purpose if it's full of administrative knick-knacks.

Renters vs. Owners

We frequently treat those lower on the organizational chart as renters versus owners. This means that we've prescribed their processes and given them very little authority to make decisions that directly impact their work, which ultimately lowers engagement and fulfillment. It sounds like the easier option because the company or manager controls the variables, and the admin person only needs to do as they are told. In a sense, it *is* easier. However, an admin will quickly grow tired, bored, or frustrated waiting to be told what to do. This is exactly what happened with our receptionists. They were bored and frustrated, feeling unseen behind the phone. Why would they be motivated to show up on time every day if they are simply occupying a rented space?

The A-players on your team want to own their house. This gives them the sense of authority, the ability to change their workflows as they see fit, and ultimately have a hand in creating opportunities. They don't want to sign a lease, they want the deed to the house. You are the bank. You have ultimate control to repossess their house. However, they want ownership. Your team wants ownership over the variables that impact their house. This helps them understand the value they add to the company. How does their purpose fit into the overall vision or mission, and why is it important? What can they personally contribute to add value to that purpose?

Transferring Ownership

Let's reevaluate our receptionist problem. Elevating the role solved our issue, but not every owner has the budget or need to move the entire role to the next level. (There are over one million receptionists in the United States, so it's clearly working somewhere.) Just as the owner of the company is invested in their business, the key to elevating the members of your admin team is by unlocking their investment mentality. How can a receptionist be invested in their role and take ownership of their house? The first step is to go through chapters three and four in this book to define the six primary workflows, title, and purpose of their house. Once you have a clear understanding of the purpose of the house and which workflows they impact, you can determine how this house fits into the bigger picture.

First, look at the purpose of the house and ask *why* this is important. Below is an example for a receptionist:

Purpose: My purpose is to quickly, professionally, and accurately filter all phone, mail, and visitor correspondence that comes into the company.

Why is this important?

- It is important that phones are answered within three rings to provide excellent customer service.

- It is important that mail is sorted and delivered to the correct person because it contains sensitive information.

- It is important that visitors are greeted professionally and attentively because a first impression sets the tone for the rest of the meeting.

The next step is to transfer **ownership** of this purpose into the receptionist's AM House.

- If your primary means of customer interaction is by phone, which part of the customer experience can the receptionist impact?

- If your receptionist must handle sensitive information in the mail, do they understand why this is important to the company's mission?

- If your receptionist is the first impression for all visitors, how can they elevate that experience to make it more memorable and increase the odds of a favorable outcome to the meeting?

When everyone in your company—right down to the receptionist—has something to own that directly contributes to the mission of the company, they buy into their position and take ownership of their AM House. When people understand why they are doing a particular task, it is more likely to be done correctly and timely. Without a *why*, your admin team will have difficulty connecting with the task and it will never be as important to them as it is to you. Remember, you understand the mission better than anyone. Communicate it to every level in a way that makes it resonate with their job duties, not just yours.

Exposure

A quick and easy way to ensure your mission resonates with your admins is to provide more opportunities for exposure to your mission. This can be in the form of a site visit, a tour through your manufacturing shop, or an opportunity to get hands-on. There is immense value in having the support roles witness the end product of your company. Many of them may be able to speak to technical aspects of what you do because they work with the documents and talk to the people directly involved in the products, but witnessing the process brings another dimension to the competency and level of ownership in everyone's mission.

At Hestel Construction, the management team schedules visits to construction sites and job shops for the administrative teams. I'm not just talking about the admin who directly supports the projects, but everyone in the HR, accounting, office management, and executive admin teams. When we make arrangements for the office staff to step away from their desks and into the mission of the company, something special happens. The accounting specialist sees the dumpsters full of demolished drywall, not just "5 pulls" typed on an invoice. The sheer size and weight of the dumpster suddenly feels worth a few hundred dollars to haul away. The human resources manager witnesses the field supervisor enforcing safety to the electricians perched on ten-foot ladders. Scheduling that safety training last month had a direct impact. The office manager sees the portable printer, laptop, and Wi-Fi hotspot she ordered, set up next to a stack of reports in the office trailer. She understands why the supervisor requested a more expensive printer. Most importantly, they see the building renovation that will repurpose an old office space into a new training facility for the U.S. Navy. There is a new sense of pride in the company, and ownership in the support they provide to their teammates who make the product.

> **You're all rowing the same boat. Everyone should have the opportunity to look left, right, forward, and back to make sure you're rowing in the same direction.**

This exposure brings a level of appreciation for the boots on the ground, but also provides exposure to experiences beyond the cubicle. Unless you're NASA, nothing you do is rocket science, it's just a matter of exposure, experience and guidance.

Give Them Authority

It's easy for upper-level management to take ownership of their responsibilities. It's easy for the front-line worker to take ownership of the product they create, or service they provide. When it comes to administrative workers, it's more difficult to identify how they impact the bottom line or the mission of the company because they work behind the scenes. This makes it doubly important that the owners and managers communicate the reasons behind the admin role's responsibilities. With clear purpose and authority, the admin person can take ownership of their house and become invested in their role—and in your mission. This clarity and authority will elevate your team's performance and reduce turnover.

A few key exercises will help create clarity around your admin team's authority. Examine the workflows and purpose of each role to identify how they impact the greater mission of the company. Put a why behind each of their primary workflows and communicate this with your staff regularly. Expose your admin people to the end product and mission of the company. Show them how their contributions directly affect the customers, vendors, or employees. Finally, examine your own house. If you are micromanaging or hoarding responsibility, reflect on how you can begin transferring ownership out of your house and into theirs.

So far, we have covered the front door of the house through hiring, the windows of the house through workflows, the address of the house through title and purpose, and the deed of the house through ownership and authority. At this point, you have a good grasp on how to design and structure your administrative team. Next, we will cover the most complex of the components: the people who occupy the house and the personalities that affect how it runs.

⛌ Next Step

Step 1

Flip to Appendix A and look around the outside of the house. There are several lines. Fill in these spaces with the other main departments in your organization. Standard departments include:

- Operations/Production
- Sales/Marketing
- Estimating/Purchasing

- Executive/Management

- Finance

- Human Resources

Only write the departments that apply to your company. If you're a small company, you may have one person filling more than one department. That's ok. Recognize that these departments still exist.

Broadening your administrative team's viewpoint of the company outside their role increases their investment in the mission of the company. When done effectively, it will increase their buy-in to your vision, and result in a more productive and engaged team.

Step 2

Schedule a time to expose your admin to the front lines of your company. Whether it's taking them out of the office to a work site or manufacturing shop, or cross-training with the frontline workers, the experience will broaden their view of their role.

"What if the admin already sees our end-product on a regular basis?" Great question. Let's pretend you're running a bakery. Your back-office admin person sees the bakery every day. They know exactly what the company makes and how they serve the customer. The key is to help them see it from another point of view. Have the admin assist with bakery prep before you open or learn the basics during a slow hour. The admin could spend an hour interacting with customers and soliciting feedback. If you're still struggling to figure out how to do this, refer to Appendix A and the departments written around the house. Look for other opportunities. Perhaps the purchasing department orders a very special ingredient from a local farmer or manufacturer. There is a great opportunity to expose your team to the source of your secret ingredient and strengthen your relationship with your vendor by scheduling a visit to their site.

The key is to get creative and help the admin person understand the greater impact of their responsibilities and how it contributes to the mission of the company. Find a way to connect the dots and your admin will become more invested in their role and the team. Think of a time and place that will help your team see their greater value and get them out of their own four walls. Mark your calendar.

CHAPTER 6

thermostat

A Stale Company

I returned to Hestel Construction after my eight-week maternity leave, refreshed and ready to jump with both feet back into my role as vice president of construction. The team was excited to have me back and my counterpart, Mike, who covered many of duties during this time, was relieved. It felt wonderful to be missed and welcomed home. That first week of March had the newness of a fresh spring day.

I had missed quite a bit during my leave. The company was neck-deep in a new acquisition—a manufacturing company, with great potential for production but severe needs in administration and management. We acquired a talented group of craftsmen who could create beautiful things from metal, but everything about the company was outdated. The stale smells of cigarette smoke, old boots, and burning metal permeated every area of the building. It was dimly lit with little separation between shop space and office space. Grease from the unmaintained machines smeared across all surfaces and metal shavings settled into corners. The neglected building was brimming with production but was weighed down with humid air and stagnant management. The temperature of the building was only controlled by the outside elements and the hot chaotic energy of production.

Aaron, the newly recruited operations executive, had experience leading and growing a manufacturing plant in Pennsylvania's steel country. He had all the knowledge of production and fabrication processes, but the administrative side of the acquisition was a mess. The makeshift offices and dividers in the front of the building were cluttered with disorganized papers, folders, samples, old phones, ancient computers, and God knows what else.

Meet Janet

Janet, the executive assistant (EA) at Hestel Construction, was always eager and willing to jump in when someone needed help. People gravitated toward her friendly and outgoing personality. She frequently joked about her OCD, keeping everything in her office "just so," with binders labeled, color coded and neatly aligned on her shelves. When the newly acquired company needed help cleaning out their offices and reorganizing, her hand shot up quickly. She volunteered to get the place in order. It was her *thing*.

Janet and Aaron worked long hours together sorting through purchase orders, filling dumpsters with odds and ends, and cleaning out the old, musty offices. She gladly helped update the technology and organize their files. Janet learned about the new business by proxy and developed friendships with the workers. Always eager to help, she didn't mind doing odd jobs around the shop or office whenever someone needed a hand.

Always supportive of growth, the owner saw this as an opportunity for Janet and promoted her to vice president of administration for the new acquisition. Pride and ego settled in fast. Janet took her new position to heart and head. She worked tirelessly to keep the parts and pieces of the business running, doing anything that needed to be done. She answered phones, taught herself to keep the books, color coded folders, and counted nickels and dimes for the shop workers to purchase snacks from a makeshift vending machine.

Janet didn't realize the leadership opportunity she was missing while she was busy trying to do everything herself. She settled into her comfort zone of doing daily tasks when the company desperately needed someone who could evaluate and restructure their administrative people and processes. Instead of instituting automation, she continued answering phones and emails. Instead of learning the software, she continued making manual forms and copies. Instead of hiring a qualified bookkeeper, she continued to keep the books herself. She hired multiple other people out of desperation, but they never stayed long. She spent day after day running around, putting out fires. By the end of the summer, it was clear she had the drive to perform, but not the skills to lead. Something had to change to move this business forward. The admin team was focused on the wrong things and was losing money quickly.

Righting the Ship

Returning from my maternity leave quickly transitioned from a fresh spring day in my nice clean office, to the stifling August heat in a stagnant and disorganized shop. My focus shifted from managing well-run construction teams to getting a handle on the hectic manufacturing team. I spent hours with Janet and Aaron, evaluating their processes and people, coaching and mentoring, helping them reorganize their team, and prioritize their goals. Aaron's knowledge of the industry was too valuable to spread him thin across departments. Janet was spending too much time functioning as a tasker instead of a leader. It was clear they needed a leader to right the ship, but it wasn't me. The owners and I debated whether to hire someone to truly run this business correctly. Their budget couldn't support it, but they also couldn't afford to continue the way they were operating.

"I'm going to throw a crazy idea out there," I said behind the closed door of the owner's office. "You have two VPs on the construction side, me and Mike. What if Mike took over the manufacturing business?"

"It's funny you say that," he replied. "Mike's already approached me about it." There must have been something in the air—our clean, conditioned office air helped us think more clearly. The answer was clear, but it wasn't going to be easy.

The Hard Conversation

After months of planning for the transition, I finally had to deliver the news to Janet. We had missed the mark on her promotion. She functioned very well as the executive assistant, but running the admin team at the new company was a poor fit. I didn't want to lose her because she was a great fit for the company. She was the right person in the wrong seat. Delivering this news—no matter how eloquently you phrase it—never lands well.

I started the explanation with a description of the company's current situation and praised her eagerness to jump in. She embraced the core values and we appreciated her dedication. But there was still hard news to deliver.

"You've been a valuable part of this team and we don't want to lose you, but we need to make a change. We need to replace our customer service manager. You already know how to do this job, and you do it well. This is where we need you, not as the VP of administration." Tears welled in her eyes and my heart sank. She viewed this as a failure, which was difficult to argue. She didn't say much to me and resigned shortly after this conversation. It wasn't a surprise. I was simultaneously sad that we'd lost her and relieved that she'd found another position where she could start fresh. This was a difficult lesson for all of us.

Lessons Learned

The question isn't *where did Janet go wrong*, the question is *where did we go wrong*. Had she continued as the executive assistant, she may still be a valuable and happy part of our team to this day. Could she have helped the new company reorganize their office? Sure. Could she have returned to Hestel Construction as the EA after a few months of helping? Yes. Could she have served in a different role at the new company from the very beginning? It's hard to tell.

Another option would have been to give Janet additional tools and mentoring prior to taking over the administrative leadership. I attempted to step in and provide these tools, but it was too little, too late. She was already in over her head. As difficult as it was, the damage was done and pulling her back was the best decision, even though it meant we lost her.

Our team was desperate to get the new company on track and made a quick decision to place Janet in a leadership role without much clarity or training. It was a short-sighted decision and we suffered through several months of poor management as a result. Janet was excited to receive a promotion and be in a leadership role. She did the best she could, but also suffered through those months with long hours, high stress, and few results to show for her efforts.

The true lessons learned are in our assessment and application of Janet's strengths. If we'd approached it more methodically, with a thorough review of her contributions to the team and natural superpowers, the decision would have been different. We would not have placed her in a broad leadership role. This is not to say she wouldn't have had opportunities for growth, but her path would be different and more aligned with her strengths. If we had analyzed the tools she would need to be successful in any new role, I suspect she would still be a contributing member of our team.

Setting the Thermostat

Spaces that we enter, both physically and metaphorically, already have some predetermined features. The musty, stale space in the manufacturing business needed a breath of fresh air that would change the temperature and bring new ideas and stability to the company. People bring their own natural superpowers and baggage to the roles they enter. Beyond their technical skills and abilities, people also bring their past experiences along for the ride. Whether it's a prior demeaning boss, low confidence, cultural differences, turbulent relationships, or any number of other factors, it influences your leadership and expectations. Taking into account natural disposition and past experiences, being crystal clear with roles and expectations is critical. This is where your admin impacts the temperature of the AM House.

Have you ever worked in an office where a single thermostat hanging on the wall is a source of tension or playful debate?

Susan likes it set at sixty-eight degrees while Mel prefers a toasty seventy-three. When Susan leaves for lunch, Mel cranks up the heat. Everyone has an optimal temperature at which they feel comfortable and most productive. While the temperature of your AM House has an acceptable range set by the company, an individual has a natural preference as well.

The Right Fit

Which comes first, the person or the role? It's a chicken and egg question, but there are two ways to consider finding the right fit for a role.

Situation One

You have the role defined, but you need the right fit. If you have an immediate role to fill and you've done the analysis on the expectations for workflows and purpose, the next step is to determine the single most important natural aptitude required to perform well in the role. Refer back to chapter two on hiring which advises you to focus more on broad expectations and less on a list of duties. Yes, you may need someone with a specific certification or knowledge base, but more importantly, you need the right fit. If this person is going to spend day after day doing data entry, finding someone with focus and attention to detail is critical, regardless of past experience. If this person needs to talk on the phone all day, they must possess strong interpersonal skills. The AM House has a preset temperature that the right admin can maintain.

Situation Two

You have a great fit for your company, but you need to find the right role for them. To do this, reverse the analysis. What is this person's natural aptitude? Where do they shine? Being great at their current job is not specific enough. Someone like Janet who is excellent at the organization of things does not translate to being excellent at the organization of people and processes. Finding your admin person's superpower and honing in on how it relates to a function in the company will provide better results than attempting to elevate someone simply to satisfy their desire for growth. It's critical to set your admin person up for success by ensuring the right fit. In this situation, the admin has a natural temperature in which they work best, and the AM House is customized to the admin.

Traps

Most people will not request a demotion. It's difficult to admit weakness and ask to be placed in a lesser role. They will either work tirelessly to get the job done to the best of their ability (like Janet) or they will leave. People like to think they make decisions based on logic, but humans are emotional creatures. We battle internal egos and crave recognition. Even when logic and results show us the rational decision, admitting failure or weakness is never easy.

When we recognize that an administrator is particularly organized, efficient, and detail oriented, we may be inclined to promote them to a management role without the training or guidance to help them make the leap from a doer to a manager. Many women in administrative roles fall into the trap of being excellent helpers. They want to help and seek the recognition that comes along with being the "go to" person. There is nothing wrong with wanting to help; we want to surround ourselves with people who are willing to put forth the extra effort to help their team succeed. The trap comes into play when we reward the helpers by elevating them from doers to leaders and expecting them to make the jump naturally, without the proper tools or support.

We want to give admin staff the skills and support they need to become great leaders and not promote for the sake of recognition. The best way to do this is to identify your natural leaders within the company. Your natural leaders are not always your best helpers and doers. When we talk about entry-level administrative professionals, we can usually separate them into two categories: producers and improvers. By understanding these two types of workers, you can more easily identify their strengths and potential for growth. Decisions about promotions and delegation of responsibilities become clearer once you've identified your producers from improvers.

Bore Them

How do you identify your top performing producers and improvers? The fastest way to separate your natural A-players from the rest is to bore them. Bore them to tears. Give them something mundane and inefficient to do and leave them to their own devices. Give them something that takes an hour and give them four hours to complete it.

If they surf the web, go on social media, and do other things unrelated to the business, they are not your A-players. I'm not condemning these time-fillers—there are moments when we all need a break. But if someone can fill a large chunk of time with personal tasks without regard for the company, they are not your A-players. They might be an A-player for someone else, but not you. They might just be there for a paycheck. The only time I recommend keeping these players is in temporary situations. If they are there to fill a void for a short time, without vested interest in their career or your business, we can let this one slide. But for your future team, let them go at the end of their temporary assignment and find your A-players.

A-players will do things a little differently. You do not need to bribe or externally motivate an A-player to fill their time with valuable contributions. They can't stand being bored, and can fill that void on their own.

Producers

Producers are A-players who understand your processes and are invested in their employment. When you bore them, they will come back to you and ask, "What's next?" Producers will require additional time and management from you or their direct supervisor for this reason. However, producers thrive in an independent, task-related position that does not require much collaboration or process improvement. When you create efficient processes, producers become supercharged. Producers are A-players who consistently move the ball forward. When you have a producer, it is important to recognize the position's requirements and determine if they are the right fit for the job. Beware of putting an effective producer in a management or leadership position. Producers are impatient and get frustrated by obstacles, which are primary challenges for managers and leaders. This can be a poor fit for true producers. This is not to stifle their growth; there are growth opportunities for producers. Producers can be subject matter experts, technical specialists and proficient employees. Producers can also handle high volume or technically demanding roles.

Improvers

On the other hand, improvers will complete the task and find additional things to do without requiring your direction. They may begin researching, poking through your files and processes, looking for better ways to do things. They may talk with another team member to glean information on why things are done a certain way. They will ask questions of themselves and others, seeking to understand the bigger picture. Improvers will fill voids with learning, growing, and improving themselves and your business. Where improvers fall short is with high volume, time-bound tasks. They can also become annoying if you don't like people asking too many questions. Think back to my stories about Spintas & Sons and working for Darrell. Frustrations arose when I asked questions and spent too much time learning instead of producing. I was in improver mode, but I was hired to be a producer—they wanted me to get the work done and not ask questions.

Producer-Improver Balance

The producer and improver types are not two buckets, they are a continuum. All A-players will fall somewhere on the continuum, leaning naturally towards producer or improver, with some being capable of both. A high performing admin team should comprise a good mix of producers and improvers. Do not hire a team of people who sit in the middle of the continuum thinking you're getting the best of both worlds. This will lead to a team of people who lack direction, where everyone is trying to do everything, and they will neither efficiently or effectively accomplish anything.

> **To create a team that is both effective and efficient, you need a balance of people who are clearly producers or improvers.**

It might look something like this: Bob is your Payroll Clerk. The door to his office is closed most days as he audits and makes sure everyone is getting paid and benefits are allocated correctly. He brings reports to you for review once a week and makes identified corrections. He files and pays the quarterly taxes. He answers questions from your workforce about their hours, benefits and paychecks. Bob is a producer.

Danielle is your office manager. She keeps the office stocked and researches vendors to find the best prices, quality, and customer service for your supplies, technology, security, and cleaning services. Others call on her to troubleshoot their phones and laptops. She brings suggestions to you about new software and basic process improvements. Danielle is an improver.

Both Bob and Danielle are critical to your admin team. As your company grows, Bob's volume of payroll will grow, and benefits and taxes may become more complex. Danielle's volume stays consistent, but there may be opportunities for her to improve your employee or vendor experiences.

Finding the Optimal Temperature

Now that you've shifted your mindset to thinking of your admin staff as they relate to the AM House, consider the influences they bring to the house. The information that lives in this house is sensitive to the conditions. Being too cold, too hot, too humid, or too dry will impact the efficiency and effectiveness in the way the information is processed. There are a few ways the admin person can change the conditions within the house. They can open or close an existing window to affect the rate at which information is exchanged. Or they can turn on a fan by modifying the steps for a specific task.

In addition to the tools that the admin brings, every house has a thermostat. The thermostat sets the baseline "temperature" for the house using the producer-improver continuum as the unit of measurement. A role that requires a producer mentality sets the thermostat to the warm side. When an improver moves in they require the thermostat to be set on the cooler side. An improver reduces the temperature, analyzes processes and freezes productivity. On the other hand, when a producer moves into an improver house, they crank up the heat, and burn through the tasks without slowing down to assess the effectiveness of the processes.

How do you find the right fit for the temperature of your AM Houses? You can predetermine the temperature of the house before bringing the admin person inside, being very clear that they must maintain the current temperature to perform successfully in the role. Or, you can take a temperature gauge of the person first, and then determine which type of house is a good match. Someone who performs well in a producer house may not have the skills or tools to adapt to an improver house. The right person will be more than just a good match with the house, they will bring fresh air to the house and tweak the conditions for optimal performance. There is always a range in which the house can operate effectively and efficiently. However, every house and every person has a magic number. If you can get the exact match— if the thermostat and the person can click into perfect alignment—magical things will happen that will make your job easier and your people happier. It takes a little work, but it's possible.

Critical for Success

The right A-player will align with the thermostat of the house, even when you're unaware. However, when you have a poor fit for the role, it becomes abundantly clear. Even when you have the right fit for the company, the wrong fit for a role will cost precious resources to you and your team.

> **Whether you're looking to fulfill a role now, or you're open for the right person to join your company, finding the right fit is critical to the success of your admin, and the efficiency of the company.**

Think of your admin roles on the producer-improver continuum. Both types of roles are equally important to keep your business running, but it's important to identify the primary condition of the role and the person. Be intentional about setting thermostats and taking the temperature of your admin to be sure your expectations align. It's not about whether a producer or an improver is a better employee, it's about the fit for the role. When the house and the person click into the just right conditions, they become your A-team. As we transition into the next chapter, having a clear understanding on how people bring their natural talents to a role will help shape your decisions to provide opportunities for growth.

🌡 Next Step

In this exercise you're going to use your diagram in Appendix A in two ways. First you will evaluate the natural disposition of the person filling the role. Then you will look at it from the perspective of what the role requires.

Refer back to your partially completed diagram in Appendix A. Working with the same person in the same house, take their producer/improver temperature. Read through the three traits listed below the admin's name from chapter two. Does this person jump out to you as a natural producer or improver? Do they crank through tasks and are always looking for what's next? Or do they analyze processes, identify efficiencies, ask questions, and research options? In your diagram, add the producer or improver symbol in the circle next to the admin's name.

Once you've decided which side of the thermostat your admin naturally sits, take a few minutes to think about the role they fill. Does the primary purpose of the role require a high volume of repetitive tasks that impact the direct output of the company? Read through the windows, title, and purpose. For example, a bookkeeper is typically a producer. They have a set process to follow, and it is repeatable for a large volume of accounts payable and accounts receivable.

Does the primary purpose of the role require research and development of opportunities to increase income, or decrease costs? For example, a marketing admin does not make the product, but researches opportunities and prepares documents for customers as an improver. In your diagram, add the producer or improver symbol in the circle next to the title. Finally, does the temperature of your admin match the intent of their role? The two circles, one near the admin's name and one near the title, will give you an indication of whether this person is a good fit for the role. If they match, you're in luck. You have an admin who is the right fit, and with some mentorship and clarity, they will shine. If they don't match, have no fear, this exercise alone is not a basis to make any rash decisions. Getting clarity on your current team's situation will better inform future decisions as you grow and the roles evolve. With a better understanding of where your people thrive best, you can make small changes along the way to provide the right opportunities for their natural talents.

CHAPTER 7

new doors

The Club

"Sam and I will be out of the office on Thursday," Brandon said. I didn't think much of this until later that day when Jim repeated the same thing, then Ryan and Rich. It occurred to me that I would be the only one left in the office. Was this just a coincidence? I checked the shared company calendar and realized there was a golf tournament scheduled for Thursday.

That explained it.

They hadn't invited me and I couldn't blame them. I wasn't a golfer. In fact, I'd only been *real* golfing once when I was sixteen. I didn't own any golf clubs, or know the first thing about a Scramble. That night I whined to my husband about how the other team members got to do things together like golf, hunt, and fish, but because I had no experience with any of these, I was never invited. They were never intentionally dismissive or exclusive. They'd made assumptions because I'd never expressed an interest in those hobbies. It was just the way it had always been. Jim was the hunter. Brandon was the golfer. Rich and Sam had the connections. The club was rounded out.

While my conversation with my husband started as whining, we chatted into the evening and I fully vocalized the repercussions of not being inside *the club*. The issue was two fold.

First, I was missing the obvious camaraderie that happens on a casual outing. They'd return from a hunting trip with stories and inside jokes. They'd commiserate about how cold it was or how much it rained. They'd talk about who had the best target shot or tease someone else about a missed shot. When they'd laugh or recount these stories in the office, I was always on the outside, smiling politely but internally envious that I didn't share any of these social connections with the men on my team. On the surface this may not seem like a business problem, but social connections build trust and shared experiences strengthen relationships. A strong team has high trust and tight bonds.

Second, I was missing the inevitable internal business discussions that happen between colleagues when they spend an entire day together without the day-to-day distractions. They don't intentionally schedule an outing with the goal of discussing the company without me. It's only natural that their shared experience at work will become a topic of discussion. Or perhaps their golf tournament included other companies that resulted in business discussions. Either way, I was missing out on these relevant discussions, and they were missing the full representation of our company. Months went by while these outings continued every so often, and I continued to smile and ask conversational questions.

When Christmas came around, my husband was particularly excited about his gift to me. He couldn't wrap it completely, so the new golf clubs stood tall and obvious beside the tree. He was giddy with anticipation for my reaction. He'd listened to my whining and understood the impact of my envy. Not only did he give me the clubs, but also scheduled private lessons so I wouldn't make a fool of myself on the course when the time came. This was my golden ticket to the club. I couldn't wait to give them a swing.

When we returned to the office after the holidays and had our casual conversations about families, dinners, kids, and gifts, I excitedly shared my news about the golf clubs and lessons. I joked about how I'd be their star player after I'd completed my lessons. They teased me about calling it a "game" instead of a "round," but I think they got the message. When the next tournament was advertised, I raised my hand high to join the team.

After only two lessons I played in my first golf tournament. Nervous that I would swing and miss the ball, Brandon reassured me that *everyone swings and misses sometimes.* My team encouraged me as I stepped up to the tee and cheered for me when my ball soared, regardless if it was the best ball or if it fell short. They happily taught me the lingo and strategy as we moved from hole to hole. I admired the seasoned golfers' effortless drives and witnessed a few duds. My assumption that every other golfer on the course would hit a good shot every time was proven wrong. Everyone swings and misses sometimes.

This story was not isolated to golf. Once I vocalized my desire to be included in outings that they'd previously assumed I'd had no interest in, more opportunities were presented to me. I went deep sea fishing and skeet shooting with the team. Not only was I included more often, but the invitations started opening to more women in the company as well.

Lessons Learned

And then I became a world renowned golfer. Just kidding. This story isn't about my opportunity and success at golf or fishing or social events. I share this story because we need to get creative about seeking opportunities for our administrative staff. Leaders don't always see the opportunities for their teams because they are busy getting things done the way they've always been done. My team didn't initially consider inviting me to these outings because I had no experience doing them, and I hadn't expressed an interest. They didn't know I'd whined to my husband in the evenings about missing out on these opportunities.

The story in my head was that I'd missed these opportunities due to my lack of skills and experience. They didn't invite me because they didn't want me there. I'd be a burden because my skill levels were not as high as theirs. Maybe I'd embarrass them at industry charity tournaments or prevent them from enjoying an outing if they had to teach me along the way. These were the stories I told myself. In reality, they hadn't considered any of this. They didn't invite me because they didn't think I wanted to go. "She has small children at home. We shouldn't expect her to leave her home at 4am for a fishing trip," or, "She doesn't like guns. She certainly wouldn't be interested in skeet shooting," and so on. The lesson I'd learned during my golf tournament was that my team fully embraced my presence on the course once they knew I was interested.

The opportunities were available, I just needed to speak up about them. There are hundreds of books to motivate the worker and encourage people to advocate for themselves. As a leader you can encourage your team to speak up about interests and opportunities, but for most people, it's difficult to initiate from the bottom up. From a leadership perspective, we need to see past our own blind spots to help create opportunities that are not so obvious.

The Importance of Opportunity

People leave companies for career advancement, opportunities, and development. It's as simple as that. If we do not keep our teams engaged by offering opportunities to grow, they will leave. Gone are the times of "Sally the Secretary" and

"Brian the Builder" who are one-career wonders. Mindsets are evolving and it's a wonderful thing. People are not satisfied doing the same tasks over and over without challenge and growth. This pushes us all to be better, and to do better.

Administrative positions in small businesses have much lower ceilings than operations and management roles. Small businesses do not need robust back office support or a complicated corporate structure. They can't afford high overhead costs. This is a tricky situation because you need your admin people, but opportunities for advancement are limited.

If you looked into a crystal ball and could see your company five or ten years from now, what would you see? Would it look exactly the same as it does today? Would you have higher revenue or larger margins? Are you selling more? Upgrading equipment or facilities? Are you more efficient, getting more done in less time? What does your team look like? Take a few minutes to visualize it. I'm not asking you to write your ten-year goals, and figure out the metrics to get there; I'm asking you to see the details in your mind's eye. Take a mental picture of a day in the life of your business a few years down the road. Zoom in on the visual details. Walk into your office or shop or virtual domain and visualize everything you want it to be. Don't worry about how you got there, just look around. Go ahead, I'll be here when you get back.

Who did you see in that picture? Were you working in the picture, or were you off on a ski trip because your team is so effective that you can finally take time off? Were people working happily in offices or did they transition to remote work with advanced technology? Were operations organized and producing high-quality or high-volume output? Were customers writing rave reviews and returning for repeat business? Were you accepting commendations in public forums or being interviewed as inspiration for new businesses? Believe it or not, your admin team had a hand behind each of these improvements.

> **Switch your thinking from needing "admin" to needing people. You don't need admin, you need people who can do administrative things.**

Most likely there are positions throughout your company that are not classified as administration, but they perform some administrative tasks. The construction foreman completes daily production reports. The welder scans in and out of job steps in an ERP system. The salesperson tracks their contacts. Everyone is capable of carrying their related administrative burden. However, this is how we are accustomed to think of that ancillary paperwork: as a burden. When the frontline worker just wants to do their job, they slough off the administrative burden to someone else. We need to create cultures where people are accountable for their related responsibilities and have the tools to complete them efficiently.

There are thousands of great books about the culture of accountability. *Extreme Ownership*, *Traction*, and *The Five Dysfunctions of a Team* are a few of the greats. The related admin paperwork may not be the worker's favorite thing to do, but they must see the importance of the requirement and embrace it as a part of their process. Once this is in place and the right people are on board, we can elevate the administrative team to have more meaningful contributions.

The team that got you to where you are today is not necessarily the team who will take you into the future. If you're looking to grow, some things will need to change. This may be a change in personnel, or a change in the way you manage your personnel. That change must start with you because that's where the power lies. The admin people who have lower level positions may not feel comfortable identifying opportunities and initiating growth for a variety of reasons. There are internal fears of failure and rejection. There are cultural expectations that prevent self-advocacy. There are systemic issues that discourage people from speaking up. We aren't afraid to elevate our admin support teams, we are afraid of who will fulfill their supporting role if we elevate them. I challenge you with this: think about the team you need to get to that five year vision. The key to getting there is already within the positions on your team. As the leader, your responsibility is to help your team identify the potential for new doors inside and outside the AM Houses.

Why We Can't Promote Sally

Sally has been answering your phones for a few years now. People love her friendly demeanor and her responsiveness to almost any request. If she doesn't know the answer, she will always point you in the right direction. Her aptitude for customer service makes her a great candidate for a sales or customer service role. Sally's boss recognizes her talents, but he can't promote her. He needs someone to answer the phones and Sally does a great job. There is no obvious reason to promote Sally and, besides, the company is on a tight budget.

"We can't afford another customer service rep," the boss rebuts. Let's challenge the boss to think a little further into the future. Sally is excellent with the customers. Her interactions may increase the percentage of repeat customers and referrals, which is a great metric for Sally to track. How many repeat customers or referrals would it take to pay the difference in Sally's salary? Could her additional pay be commission-based, adding no additional cost to the company for Sally's promotion? It provides evidence of her added value on the sales team.

> **We aren't afraid to elevate our admin support teams, we are afraid of who will fulfill their supporting role if we elevate them.**

"But then who will answer our phones?" the boss asks. Surely, no one can replace Sally. Right? Here, again, is an opportunity for added value. The company can move to an automated phone system or directory. Some companies are abandoning landlines altogether and moving to direct cell phone contacts.

"No, we have a reputation for personal attention," the boss argues. "I want a real person answering our phones." Sure thing, boss. How about a virtual receptionist? This could maintain the intimacy of a person answering the phone while saving money compared to an office-bound receptionist. Virtual assistants and people who work from home can receive training and scripting from Sally to provide the same personal feel as a receptionist in the office. After all, the caller doesn't know that your virtual receptionist isn't in the office.

"No way. They won't understand our business the way Sally does," he continues. This is where Sally's value is apparent. We can't elevate Sally because she is *too good* at her job. Sally is stuck. What's a company to do with a stuck Sally?

There will be a tipping point where the company can't afford *not* to promote Sally. It may not happen tomorrow or next month, but at some point, Sally will be offered an opportunity. If her company doesn't offer it, someone else will. After all, Sally interacts with many industry professionals simply by answering the phones. Unfortunately, Sally's position is too common and too convenient for companies. Let's take a look at how you can help the *Sallys of the world* get unstuck.

Opportunities From Inside the House

The easiest way to identify opportunities for your A-players is from inside a well-constructed house. This is the classic example of an A-player excelling at their job, having capacity and desire for growth and seeking opportunities to add value to the company.

I once read a quote that said, "Windows bring(s) you closer to the things you love." I saw this and thought, "Yes! That's the opportunity. When we're working in our AM Houses and managing our workflows, the windows bring us closer to opportunities for growth." Now, I'm taking this entirely out of context because it was a quote about Microsoft Windows. However, in my mindset, I instantly made the connection to the AM House.

The A-player who is seeking more opportunity can look through the windows in their house and make connections. They can see a need and a means to fill it. They can reach up to the window sill and pull it down, extending the window like a mouth opening wider. It changes the opening from a window to a door. The workflow, in which the A-player participated, becomes a door they can walk through.

Sarah was an A-player with a long tenure at her company. She had started with the company as an admin assistant and slowly added responsibilities to her plate and learned new skills over the years. Working in the small office gave her proximity to the project team, from which she gleaned technical information about her company's products and services. Over the years she accumulated historical knowledge of the company's processes. One of her workflow windows was assembling project packages for the field teams. As she assembled the information, she read through the project data, and taught herself about each one. When the field staff called with questions, she could answer them instead of forwarding the call to the management team. She studied the schedules and budgets, asked questions, and anticipated changes. She reached up to the metaphorical window and pulled it down to create her door. This new door led her to a position on the project management team.

Sarah is a great example of an A-player creating new doors. We all know a "Sarah." Sarahs are a pleasure to have on your team; they perform well and are self-motivated. When you have a Sarah on your team, you don't have to be an exceptional leader to help her grow. She will find a way to grow inside, or outside, your organization. Fortunately, Sarah was loyal to the company and waited for the opportunity to present itself, then asked the leader to guide her into a new role.

Your exceptional A-players will identify and create these windows of opportunity. Your loyal A-players will wait for these windows of opportunity. Unfortunately, small businesses are jam-packed with *confused* A-players who may need a little help. Needing help to identify the internal opportunity does not mean they are subpar employees or that they are lacking motivation. Sometimes they just don't know what they don't know, and a little coaching can help them see the potential. Perhaps there are opportunities coming down the pipeline that you can see as the leader, but your A-player cannot see from within their AM House.

> **Your job is to open the blinds, push away the curtains, or open a skylight so they can see a new perspective. Show them their potential and be crystal clear about the future needs of the company.**

If you've ever thought, "That person is really going somewhere. They have so much potential," then for goodness' sake, tell them. They cannot read your mind and may be making up an entirely different story in their head. Even the most talented among us wrestle with self-doubt. When I think back to my most influential mentors, the common thread wasn't my skills, it was my mentor's ability to bring out the best of my skills. They believed in me and provided the encouragement that gave me the confidence to seek out new opportunities. Don't just pat your A-players on the back for the great things they've done, show them the greatness they can become.

Opportunities from Outside the House

Guiding your A-players from outside the house is easier for you than mentoring them from the inside. From the outside of the house you have a clear picture of the company and the roles that need to be filled. However, where owners and managers trip up is in failing to extend the opportunities across departments. Departments typically operate in silos, or in our case, separate groups of houses. Think about a real silo; you cannot penetrate the walls of the silo to travel to another silo.

The farmer does not mix materials between silos. The whole idea of a silo is to store large amounts of a specific material so that it is protected from outside elements. What goes in the silo stays in the silo until it is ready to be used. Nothing else goes in, and nothing else comes out.

The benefit to visualizing your teams in houses, instead of silos, is the ability to build connections between them. An A-player with the ability to visit other houses has opportunities to learn new skills, obtain information and build relationships. Silos do not connect or have doors leading to other silos. Your houses are strong and stable, but you have the ultimate control to alter, build and expand the houses. Creating new doors and new houses is not an overnight decision, but it is possible.

I frequently saw Latisha sitting in other people's offices for a chat. She got her work done and spent a few minutes here and there visiting offices outside her own administrative hallway. Her position supported the project management team, but she never hesitated to pop into the accounting, human resources or executive offices to ask a question. She was curious about their projects and processes, learning about other areas of the business from her genuine interest, not selfish gain. People enjoyed chatting with Latisha—she was down-to-earth, easy to talk to, and eager to understand. She was relatively new and not the top performer on her team, but she did the work.

After only six months with the company, we saw an opportunity for Latisha. We needed to add someone to the human resources department. Latisha's resume listed human resources experience. Her engagement with her coworkers was a clear sign that she enjoyed the HR side of business, and a quick conversation confirmed that she was interested in returning to human resources. This HR opportunity did not come in the form of a promotion. It was a lateral move offering the same salary and benefits with a different set of responsibilities. Despite the lack of incentive, she jumped at the opportunity to be in a position where she felt more at home.

The opportunity didn't end there. She embraced the new HR role and it was clear that she enjoyed her work. Her new role required that she engage with various people across the company, which was where she thrived. We still found her frequenting many offices and asking questions. She excited everyone with her suggestions for improvement, and her willingness to dive into processes that were previously neglected.

Then, we lost Latisha's boss, our primary HR manager. At an emergency meeting of leadership and HR staff, anxiety was running high. Not only did we have a role to fill, but there were time-critical responsibilities to cover, such as payroll. This wasn't something that could wait. We listed everything that needed to be delegated out to the team. One by one, the tasks were picked up and gaps were filled. The plan only covered the bare necessities for the next couple of weeks until we could form a permanent plan. The plan wasn't sustainable and HR needed a leader.

Latisha was eager to take the reins. When we put a temporary plan in place to fill the void, Latisha jumped in and took the lead. She wasn't looking for a promotion, she was simply passionate about what she did and would make sure the department didn't flounder. Previously we did not see Latisha's leadership qualities because she was busy learning. Once the pathway was clear, Latisha was able to take everything she had learned and accelerate quickly. She handled employee issues sensitively and fairly. She took initiative to research new regulations and make recommendations. She identified and corrected previous mistakes and navigated them carefully with the employees they affected. Once she had the right opportunity, she shined.

Latisha would have been content in her original position supporting project management. She had the brains to understand it and the focus to get it done. However, she needed a clear pathway to step into her highest and best talents. Because Latisha had already spent time visiting the other AM Houses, she had a library of knowledge about the company and individuals which made her transition to HR smooth and accelerated. Once we presented her with a new AM House on the HR team, it became her home where she continued to build and customize a fulfilling and lasting career.

Managing through silos would have put us in a position to hire a new HR admin person instead of reaching across departments to engage Latisha in the initial opportunity. It may seem obvious because Latisha had prior experience in HR, but the reality is resumes are typically filed away and never revisited after a person is hired. Latisha did not go around the office talking about her HR experience or expressing a desire to switch departments, but the leaders were keenly observant.

If Latisha operated in a silo, she would not have spent time visiting with and learning from others in the office. The management team would not have seen her engaging across departments and would have assumed she was "at home" on the project team.

Give Your A-Players Ways to Improve

Providing internal opportunities for development differentiates the growing small businesses from the stagnate small businesses. Opportunities are not just for the managers and front lines, but for the back of the house administration teams as well. When you see an increase in volume, want to diversify your business, expand your product line or services, don't overlook the untapped potential residing in your business. When you surround yourself with A-players, they are always looking for ways to improve. If you don't provide those opportunities, your best players will go elsewhere.

Opportunities for advancement come in many forms and it takes a creative and intuitive leader, *like you*, to recognize and coach for those opportunities in your admin team. Windows inside the AM House can be stretched and converted into doors, inviting your admin people to step through and either expand their existing house, or walk through to a new house, like Sarah. Opportunities that exist outside the AM House require your dedicated communication and vision to push back the curtains and show your admin what lies in the distance, like Latisha. Knowing where the company is going and communicating that to your entire organization is a way to push back the curtains so they can see what's coming next. That clarity will bring about additional ideas and new opportunities for your admins to contribute beyond the current walls of their AM Houses, and possibly, beyond their administrative department.

As you begin preparing your admin staff for new opportunities, you will naturally ask yourself how to guide them into the roles where they can have the greatest impact. But what if they're not ready? Don't give up on them. Next we'll tackle mentoring.

◌ Next Step

Again, let's use your admin example from the diagram in Appendix A. By now you should have an idea of their best traits, workflows, potential purpose statement, and an idea of their producer/improver disposition. Referring to our diagram in Appendix A, you have already constructed the main features of their house. You've identified their windows, created an address for the house, and set the thermostat.

Now comes the hard part. Without making any commitments, identify the different opportunities around the diagram. Go crazy with it and list them—no matter how outlandish—under the magnifying glass symbol along the side of the diagram. Look inside the house at the workflows and look for where you can turn a workflow into a new position. Read through the departments listed around the outside of the house for what's on the company's horizon. Look at the person's title and try putting the word *senior, manager,* or other descriptors around the title to elevate the role. Look at their producer/ improver disposition and think of another role that requires the same temperature and related skills in other departments.

Brian the Bookkeeper's list looks like this:

- From his payroll window: Payroll Specialist Extraordinaire
- From the company's future vision: Financial Controller
- From his title: Senior Bookkeeper
- From his producer disposition and outside departments: Purchasing Agent

I understand that some people are reluctant to write down promises they can't keep and this might feel a lot like a promise to your admin. Brian the Bookkeeper may not be qualified to be a financial controller or purchasing agent at this time. Remember that this diagram is your practice space, not your business plan. Going through the exercise alone (no matter how outlandish the list), helps open your mind to identify and create opportunities. Do not hesitate to write down opportunities that are not immediately available—or that may never be. You may find that simply contemplating some impossible paths for your admin person leads to more realistic discussions, and eventually, more opportunities.

CHAPTER 8

bracing the house

Fork in the Road

Kasey had a choice to make. Hestel Construction was growing and opportunities were abundant. Kasey had worked her way up through the ranks in administration and was interested in making the leap to operations. Then, there was a fork in the road.

"A year ago you expressed an interest in becoming a project engineer," I started. "We have that opportunity now, and I have no doubt you have the knowledge and willingness to learn this position. Is this something you're still interested in?" "Yeah..." she hesitated and looked at the floor. Kasey's internal struggle was evident. She was excelling in her role as the proposal coordinator, a largely administrative role, and unsure if she was ready to hang it up for the chance to dive into operations.

"Huh," she let out a nervous laugh and paused. "I am...," she took a deep breath. "....I am so flattered that you think I could do this. But I also really like my current role. This is hard." We continued the conversation about her future. The question wasn't about the tasks she wanted to perform tomorrow, the question was about where she wanted to go. The project engineer role would take her through the ranks of project management over time. The proposal coordinator role had the potential to expand and evolve with the needs of the company in ways that were not as clear or linear as project management. At the end of the day, it was a choice between construction operations and business administration.

Kasey slept on her decision and wrestled with it over the weekend. I had been mentoring her and supporting her interest in operations for three years. She'd listened to my conversations with customers and subcontractors while I negotiated prices and debated changes. She'd watched me build schedules and asked questions when I adjusted budgets. Selfishly I was flattered by her interest in my role, and guided her along a similar trajectory. If she chose operations, it would confirm that my mentorship worked. It would confirm that I'd made operations interesting or inspiring. But this wasn't about me. I was afraid that if she didn't take the operations role, she would eventually hit a lower ceiling in administration.

The Choice

When she returned on Monday, I was anxious to hear her decision. Would she choose to follow in my footsteps or blaze her own administrative path?

She folded her hands in her lap, sat a little taller and nervously cleared her throat. "This was a hard decision, but I've decided to continue in the proposal coordinator role. I enjoy being involved in multiple divisions of the company, and I think the proposal role will give me more opportunities to stay involved."

My ego took a gut punch, but deep down I knew she made the right decision. The administrative ceiling is lower in most construction companies, but we were not like most construction companies. Hestel Construction was growing. We didn't know what her path could look like, but Kasey's determination and innovative ideas would allow her to mold it to suit her strengths and identify the opportunities for her— and the company's—growth.

Lessons Learned

My experience in construction shaped the way I'd mentored Kasey and influenced my perception of operations versus administration. I wanted to steer her away from administration because typical small construction companies did not offer opportunities for growth in administration. In my experience, most construction admins hit a low ceiling and stay there for the duration of their careers. I knew Kasey had more to offer, and I knew she would not be content in a static role for too long.

I'd let my experiences shape my expectations instead of letting her unique talents shape them. Our company was dynamic and she saw the potential in her position to shift and grow with the company. I wouldn't change a thing about the way I'd mentored her. However, I would change the way I'd applied my experiences in other companies to the expectations of Kasey's role. I should not have been disappointed that she wouldn't choose the same path I chose. It was not evidence of failure on my part. It was evidence that she had the confidence in the company to continue to break the molds of old-school construction and restore respectability and opportunity to administrative positions. She had shined a light on my administrative blind spot.

Mentorship

I am using the term mentor to encompass all roles that support the career path of another. This can be a mentor, sponsor, coach, etc.

Mentorship is not about teaching someone to do things the way you do them. It's about helping them discover their own voice. It's about teaching tools they can use for their own growth. Don't be surprised if they use the tools differently than you do—the important part is that you've provided the tool and shown them one way to use it. They may flip that tool upside down to use it in an entirely new way. Even if you haven't spent time in an administrative role, that should not prevent you from mentoring your admin person. Mentoring in leadership, mindset, and goal setting is applicable to everyone.

You may or may not have the perfect mentors in your company for your admin staff. You can still provide opportunities for your admins to seek mentors outside of your company by encouraging them to join an industry association or have them spend time with a partner company. I personally prefer in-person connections, but there are plenty of virtual groups who can also offer mentoring and coaching. There are blogs, books, and LinkedIn groups where your A-players can learn, ask questions and connect with others.

> **Mentorship is not about teaching someone to do things the way you do them. It's about helping them discover their own voice.**

Brace Their House

One of my motivating objectives for writing this book is to open the minds of leaders to the opportunities within administration. This is where things get tricky. I could have written the book for the administrators, to give them tools to add value to their companies and encourage confidence so they can reach further for new opportunities. Essentially you could have put the responsibility of mentorship on me. (Just as mentioned above, A-players can seek mentors through books.) However, you, as the leader, still have a key role to play. The ability to level-up the admin team relies on the leaders, managers, and owners within the company to provide support for the growth of their staff. The number one reason people voluntarily leave their positions is for career advancement and growth.

As mentioned in chapter five, your goal for the admin is to take ownership of their house. If they feel the ownership, they will want to put in the blood, sweat, and tears to customize that house. They have the power to customize the interior of their AM House and build additions onto it. Customizing the interior is adding their ideas, efficiencies, and flare to the workflows they control. Growth can come in the form of building new rooms, adding a balcony, or expanding the space. As a mentor and leader, your job is to provide support and tools for success in their original AM House while they develop the skills to renovate and upgrade the existing area.

Imagine a friend who inherited their parents' house built in the 1960s. You remember visiting this house as a child when it felt like an inviting home with toys, games, and most importantly, your friend. Visiting your friend's house was always more exciting than staying at home and you remember this house fondly. You return to it twenty years later. The parents have passed away and your friend must decide whether to sell it or keep it. When you walk in, you see it for the first time through modern eyes. The wood paneling makes the rooms look dark and small. It's hard to imagine kids playing games on the worn and matted carpeting. The low ceilings make it feel cramped and you instinctively duck while passing through each doorway. The windows are small and sealed shut with layers of cracked and peeling paint, preventing fresh air from circulating through the house. Regardless of whether they will be selling or inhabiting the house, this place clearly needs some work.

Your friend decides to move in while renovating it at the same time. The house has sentimental value and a lifetime of memories. They can't imagine anyone else buying the house just to change it into something unrecognizable. Your friend is handy and can do most of the interior facelift themselves. When it comes time to do some heavy lifting, you are there to help. You help hang dust barriers and lay down protective sheets to cover the raw subfloor. These efforts make sure the livable space is protected from the dust and debris of the renovation.

This physical protection is critical for your friend to live comfortably in the primary space of the house, just as it's critical for your admin person to protect their primary duties as they learn new skills. You don't need to block and tackle the dust yourself, you just need to help them define their boundaries and place protective barriers. This is the first step in bracing the house.

When it comes time to do some major renovation you can help your friend in two ways. You can physically construct the new space with your friend *or* you can give them the resources to hire a contractor. Physically building with your friend is the equivalent to directly mentoring your admin. If you have the time and experience, you may enjoy this hands-on work. It can be difficult at times, but is immensely rewarding. It gives you the opportunity to customize the house and ensure the house is properly supported while new structures are built.

If you don't have the time, skills or experience to put in, you can help your friend hire someone who does. Through your network you could refer a good home renovator to your friend. You may help fund the effort, or simply help them make contact. Whether you physically help your friend build or you provide the resources for them to hire a contractor, you've reinforced their efforts and accelerated the improvement of the house.

Even when you don't directly provide the mentorship, supporting the effort and bracing their house are just as important. As the leader, you need to decide if there are association dues or paid time during the workday that require your approval to support the mentorship. Whether you provide direct mentors within your company or help your admin find outside resources, you play an important role in bracing their AM House.

The Mentor-Mentee Relationship

Some companies have an official mentoring program. If you have one, great. You're a step ahead of most small businesses. I am not here to teach you how to implement a mentorship program, but I am here to give you the reasoning behind ensuring your A-players have access to a mentor. There are many resources out there on how to begin a mentorship program in your company. Plenty of books are available to step you through it. Other companies offer consulting services that provide in-depth guidance and support for these programs. It is up to you to decide if a structured program is the best fit for your company or if you prefer to allow a casual and natural evolution.

Whether you implement it yourself or use a professional service, let it naturally flow or follow a structure, one of the key steps is matching the mentor to the mentee. The mentor-mentee relationship is deeply personal and when matched well, deeply valuable. You cannot force a mentor onto someone and expect personal investment in the relationship. This is not an arranged marriage. Inspiring bosses will naturally attract followers who look to them as a mentor. I have experienced many of those relationships as the mentee and can speak to the intrinsic motivation and heightened performance that results from a well-formed mentor-mentee relationship.

You might be the most inspiring person with all the best intentions, but there will still be some personalities that won't click with yours. And that's ok. You don't need to be everyone's mentor. What's more important is the comfort level between the mentor and mentee. Ultimately, the mentee chooses their mentor. Your job is to give them access to mentors. Brace their house by supporting the relationship and allowing time in your admin's schedule to meet with the mentor.

> **The mentor-mentee relationship is deeply personal and when matched well, deeply valuable.**

Promotion versus Growth

If you're going to invest in a home renovation, why not just build a newer, bigger, shinier house? If you're going to invest in growing your admin people, why not just give them a promotion? More pay, more responsibility, less stress on you. By all means, if your company is growing, and you need someone in a higher level role and your admin is the right fit, promote them. And once they've moved into the newer, bigger house, decide if you need a new admin to occupy their old house, or if it gets renovated, abandoned, or demolished.

I recognize that not all small businesses can support their admin by building new houses and handing out promotions. And not all admin staff are ready for a new house. Growth in the form of mentorship is a way to encourage rewards in your admins. Whether you're ready to invest in promotions or not, the key to leveling up your admin team is giving them the tools and support they need to feel intrinsically motivated to give *you* their best efforts and ideas. Bracing their house for internal growth is a great way to do this.

Your A-players do not necessarily need extra money and more tasks to feel valued. Money is great, but if you're already compensating them fairly, more money does not motivate A-players to perform at their best. Dedicating time, resources and support will set up your A-players for top performance and growth.

We All Need a Good Mentor

All employees need a good mentor. It is really up to the employee to choose a mentor who will inspire them and support their goals. As a great boss who is invested in the development of your team, there is no doubt that some will choose you. In these cases, brace their house by protecting their time and the resources associated with their original position, and invest your time and resources to help them expand their house. Sometimes your admin will choose a mentor other than you, but your job is still to protect the original purpose of their house as they seek guidance and inspiration from their mentor. Finally, there will be some admin staff who are unsure where to find a mentor. Do not leave these admin lost and lonely in their house. In these cases, provide them with resources outside the company for them to connect with other admin professionals or inspiring leaders in your industry. Assigning a mentor has some benefits, but ultimately the mentor and mentee must click. If you've had an impactful mentor in your life, you understand the importance of a good mentor-mentee relationship.

The importance and benefits of mentorship extend well beyond the four walls of the AM House. Mentorship does not just benefit the mentee by adding to their network, but it increases their capacity, motivation, and investment. When your admin team performs at their best, they level-up to become your A-team. When the house is built and supported, their performance will soar. In a perfect world—and with some practice—you will be able to build and support these strong houses for optimal performance. However, there are stigmas and stereotypes that will show up occasionally as cracks in their foundation. We will explore these next so you can be identify and patch them before they threaten the stability of your admin team.

> **When your admin team performs at their best, they level-up to become your A-team. When the house is built and supported, their performance will soar.**

🚶 Next Step

Some admin staff are clear on their mentor. Others might lean on a family member or close friend for support, but lack a career mentor. If your company is very small, your staff may think that you are their only option. The goal of this exercise is to document the mentor who is crystal clear, and to identify a few resources for admin staff who need help finding a mentor.

If your admin seems a bit isolated with little support, provide them with links to industry associations or virtual career groups so they can find and choose a mentor.

In your house diagram in Appendix A, identify the person on the outside of the wall. If you already know that your admin has a clear mentor, write the mentor's name next to this person. If you're unsure of the mentor, leave it blank. Either way, in the three dots under this person's name, write three ideas for resources or ways you can support that mentorship. This can be an association, a referral, a book, a mastermind group, your friend's company in a similar industry, protecting their schedule, or any other resource where they could find a mentor with a little bit of effort. Whether it's an individual name or a resource, you are bracing their house.

CHAPTER 9

cracks in the foundation

The Helpful Admin

"She keeps us all straight around here," Charlie proudly boasted of his administrator, Savannah. Charlie managed a satellite office and a staff of thirteen construction professionals, including Savannah. Her role was to manage the contract documents and maintain the project accounting. Savannah also picked up the office responsibilities of ordering supplies, answering random questions, and calling the service providers when the internet went down or the copier needed servicing. She enjoyed being the helpful admin, and keeping them all straight.

Her prescribed job duties were very specific to construction operations, but many random tasks fell into her lap. If she didn't order more printer ink, who would? As the only admin and the only woman in the office, she became the helpful, catch-all admin. The more she volunteered to be the helpful admin, the more the team leaned on her.

The men on the team appreciated Savannah. "Savannah never stops! Sometimes we're not sure if she even went home the night before," the men would tease her. Their comments were always well-intentioned and they wanted to shine a spotlight on Savannah for her hard work and dedication to the team.

At first, Savannah felt valued, knowing that the team relied on her for more than just data entry. She worked tirelessly to stay on top of her prescribed duties and respond to every random request from the team. After a year of being the catch-all around the office, she told me, "I can't take a day off. This office will be chaos without me and I'll come back to a mess. I don't want that stress so I try not to take any time off." Savannah loved her job, but she was exhausted.

Lessons Learned

Savannah's role was initially built in a strong house. The company had a standard blueprint for her role that was stable and secure in other offices. She had a clear purpose and title, her workflows followed documented processes, and she had the drive to be successful. What happened? Over time, the team and circumstances chipped away at her foundation.

The team was allowed to cut new windows into her walls. A sprinkle of requests became a deluge over her house. She did her best to prop up her structure and manage new windows. She placed buckets under the leaky roof to catch each request that came through, but her foundation began to crack.

In an office full of men, it's typical to see a female admin in a support role. She has a desire to belong to the team and finds her value in becoming the caretaker, responding to any reasonable request. The trouble with this is knowing when to draw the line. The helpful admin does not want to say "no" to her boss or turn down an opportunity to add value to the team. The more she accepts, the more the men lean on her for the small duties they don't feel like doing. One favor to pick up coffee on her way into the office becomes a weekly errand.

Savannah also had a desire to learn and grow with the company. However, she was so inundated with additional tasks, she had no time to take classes or work with a mentor. Her plate was overflowing—leaving no room for learning, growing, or problem solving. It was as if there were keys to more opportunities hanging on the wall of her house, but they were out of reach. There were too many miscellaneous tasks coming through her windows and cluttering her space and she couldn't find the stepstool to reach the keys.

Lastly, Savannah's salary was commensurate with other administrators in the company and throughout the industry. However, her salary was half the average of the other men in her office. There were standard reasons for the men's higher salaries: years of experience, higher level responsibilities, authority to make project-level decisions, and relationships with outside vendors and customers. Furthermore, raising her salary meant raising the salary for ten other admin staff, which would add significant costs for the company.

The onus does not lie on Savannah's shoulders. She is fulfilling her primary responsibilities and supporting her team in the way that was designed by her supervisor. Savannah tries hard to hide her frustration because she wants to be seen as a team player. She feels valued when her supervisor leans on her for additional support. There is no ill intent to prevent Savannah from growing or becoming more efficient. However, there is a lack of focus on her role and the cracks in her foundation fell into this blindspot. As a leader, you have the responsibility to inventory, protect, and make sure your admins' houses are properly maintained.

Value of Administration

Operations and sales are functions of a business that drive revenue and directly impact the bottom line. After all, the business is about selling the product or service. To do that, we must create the product or service, find our customers and ultimately deliver results. The front line workers of the business receive recognition when things are going well. They get the attention and additional resources when owners want to drive sales.

If administration doesn't drive revenue, how do we make a case for its importance? They are typically lumped into the profit and loss statement as overhead or general and administrative (G & A) expenses. They appear to have zero impact on the gross profit, and have a negative impact on the net profit. The only way to increase the bottom line *without increasing revenue* is to cut costs. If your administration is on the chopping block as a means to increase profit, it's difficult to convince the team that they are valuable. Where does their value lie?

Thinking of your administrative team as overhead shifts focus away from their value and makes them an afterthought. We know they are necessary, but we invest the bare minimum to hire, train, and retain them. After all, they are a G & A expense that takes away from our profit. The startup entrepreneur may have been doing all of the administration themselves, and it's painful to add a large G & A expense in the form of additional salaries.

> **When managers and owners view administration as the people who keep things organized and clean up messes in the background, they are missing a huge opportunity. Administrators are the creators and protectors of your basic processes and systems. Well-designed and maintained processes and systems drive companies to scale up.**

Think of it like framing a house. Whether you're in the construction industry or not, we've all seen a house under construction at some point. When it's finished you have painted walls, finished floors, shiny fixtures, and a decorative façade. The end product is the beautiful finish and functional spaces of the home. However, beneath the drywall, paint, carpet, and fixtures is a strong framework. The wooden framing starts on a solid foundation and builds height to the walls. Wooden two-by-fours are not as expensive as solid brick, but are strong—and necessary—for building height when structured correctly. The carpenter builds the basic shape for the house, though it's not the finished product, **it's the system beneath the walls to which all pieces attach.** As the builder adds drywall and finishes to the wooden studs, the house takes shape. The taller the house, the higher the builder needs to extend the framework. When someone wants to build a second floor addition, they do not simply extend the drywall without framing the walls. Unsupported drywall would collapse. Likewise in your company, you must build your administrative framework to support future growth. And that framework must sit on a solid foundation.

Efficient and effective administration is as important to your bottom line as selling your product. When your frontline workers do not have a strong framework of support, they will not perform at their best. Time will be wasted navigating inefficient processes. Resources will be spent fixing mistakes. Risks will be exposed. All of these will directly impact your revenue and gross profit. The question is: do you have a strong framework of administration that is efficient and effective, or are there cracks in the foundation?

Crack 1: Gender

There are millions of administrative assistants in the US—82% of whom are women.[10] They traditionally fill support roles and the business world accepts and expects this. If we elevate women from support roles, there is a systemic fear about who will fulfill them. I don't think there is discomfort around powerful women if they are supportive or nurturing; we see examples of powerful mothers and grandmothers in many cultures.

It's no coincidence that supporting administrative roles are typically held by women. Let's take another look at Savannah's situation. She was the only woman in an office of twelve men who routinely leaned on her for domestic tasks. They all thought highly of Savannah and wanted to support her growth. However, if she was elevated from her current role, *who would pick up the tasks she left behind?* Out of fear, discomfort, or sheer convenience, they never fixed her foundation, boarded up her miscellaneous windows, or tidied up so she could finally reach the keys to the next level.

This issue is doubly prevalent in small businesses compared to large businesses. In large businesses, there are elaborate

---

10   Zippia, "Administrative Assistant Demographics And Statistics In The US," accessed 22 March 2022, https://www.zippia.com/administrative-assistant-jobs/demographics/.

corporate structures, policies, and programs that protect roles and provide clear paths of growth. Check these boxes, get that certification, maintain this tenure, and you're eligible for the next rung on the ladder. Large businesses have is policies and processes that take gender out of the equation on a surface level. There are still systemic issues in large businesses, but the prescribed framework makes it easier to avoid blatant subjectivity or discrimination. Small businesses rely on more subjective decisions when it comes to hiring, firing, and promoting—landing women in most supporting roles without paths for growth.

Whether the bias is unconscious or conscious, systemic or individual, the statistics don't lie. The good news is that small business owners and managers have a more direct impact over the diversity of their team. It takes a little extra effort, thought, and money from the small business leader to delineate growth opportunities for their administrative teams, but when it's done with clear and honest intentions, it pays dividends.

Crack 2: Fair Compensation

Perhaps the most difficult drawback for admin roles is fair compensation. Most administrative roles pay far less than the roles they support. In 2020, the average hourly wage in the United States for an office administrator was nineteen dollars and seventy-one cents per hour. This equates to an annual salary of $40,990.[11] In my opinion, this should be the minimum and not the average. Along with teachers, healthcare workers, and other frontline workers, there is a systemic disconnect between the effort and risk, and compensation for valuable and necessary careers.

In Savannah's case, the roles she supported required a higher level of experience and credentials. Yet they could not perform their roles effectively or efficiently without her. This is something I've wrestled with in my career as both the admin and the team leader. The situation varies from team to team, and company to company, and I do not have a prescription to solve it across the board. However, I will say that minimum wage is just that, a minimum, and I do not advise investing the bare minimum when it comes to the structure that supports your business. Elevate your full-time administrative personnel to a living wage. Show them that they are a valuable contributor, and not just a minimal necessity.

Crack 3: Creativity

When we think of administration, creativity is among the last words that come to mind. When we think about admin, we typically think of prescribed processes, repeatable tasks, and answering requests. However, humans are inherently emotional and creative creatures. Putting someone in a box

---

11   Occupational Outlook Handbook, "Secretaries and Administrative Assistants," Bureau of Labor Statistics, U.S. Department of Labor, Accessed February 22, 2022, https://www.bls.gov/ooh/office-and-administrative-support/secretaries-and-administrative-assistants.htm.

to perform the same tasks over and over reduces them to unthinking, unfeeling robots. There is a whole person in your admin role who has thoughts and ideas well beyond their daily tasks.

How do you foster creativity within admin roles? Creativity comes in many forms. We think of artists, musicians, novelists, actors, and philosophers. We think of our crazy Uncle Larry with his unruly hair, who is always pitching a conspiracy theory at the Thanksgiving table. We rarely think of our office managers and payroll processors. Admin roles tend to be filled by people who enjoy organization and structure. This supports the stigma that administrative roles are task driven and have no room for creativity.

Remember Kasey and her big decision? She was a high performing admin that decided to stay the course in her growing administrative role. Kasey had the organization, initiative, and attention to detail that we appreciate in our administrative teams. Others on the team trusted her and frequently visited her office for a casual chat, to ask questions, or to vent. As she grew more comfortable in her role and absorbed her colleagues' feedback, she identified the need for a focused effort on employee engagement. She took the initiative to organize a committee who not only celebrated birthdays, but added more touchpoints for the team and customized their recognition. During one particular luncheon, she designed the theme around the current Olympic games. Speaking into a toy microphone, she presented homemade metals to recognize specific employees. This was not recognition for exceeding metrics or outstanding performance. There were no bonuses or plaques on the wall for employees of the quarter. Her recognition was about comradery. She superimposed their faces on Olympic photos and gave everyone an hour of celebration and comedy.

Given the freedom to identify needs in the company and explore creative solutions, Kasey renewed the bond within the team. It was not a hefty investment for the company— only costing a few boxes of pizza. It was clear that creating the event brought joy to Kasey, and added value to the people she recognized, no matter the budget. The rest of the team appreciated the break in the day for some humor, pizza, and good company.

We assume that good admins are task driven and lack creativity. However, when given a little freedom, you might be surprised by their creativity outside their immediate area of responsibility.

Inspecting the House

When new homes are built or renovations are done, various inspections are required to ensure the construction of the home is compliant with code requirements. This ensures safety and stability for the longevity of the home. An inspection does not guarantee that things will never go wrong, but it validates the strength of the house, and prevents defects and failures under normal circumstances. Barring a natural disaster or other extreme circumstance, testing and inspections prevent cracks in the foundation.

Building your administrative team with the Adminnovate Model gives you the engineered blueprint. When done correctly, your houses will pass all tests and inspections and hold strong with basic maintenance for years to come. Every structure should be inspected periodically for cracks in the foundation so they can be mended while they are still small fissures. A small crack can widen and spread very quickly when left unattended. Appendix B (and downloadable at jamievanek.com/bonuses) is an inspection checklist that will ensure your AM Houses remain strong for years to come. I recommend including this checklist as part of your annual reviews so it does not feel like an extra thing to track. With a well-maintained home, you should be able to run through the checklist in just fifteen minutes. However, if you or your admin person identify any deficiencies, take the time to put a plan together to patch the cracks. A little time now will save you hours in the future.

In Savannah's situation from the beginning of the chapter, she was not able to patch the cracks on her own. It required buy-in and a dedicated effort from her immediate supervisor to clarify the areas of responsibility amongst the team. Savannah could not simply refuse to help when someone made a request of her time outside her primary duties. Casual complaints and comments about the added work did not get the attention of her team. When someone asked for her help, she explained her purpose which bought her some time, but it didn't prevent the requests from coming. She needed a thorough inspection of her role and the roles of others in the office to uncover the root of the issue. There was an antiquated culture where it was ok to lean on the helpful admin for all requests that were not deemed important enough for the men. The cultural shift had to come from the leader to shore up Savannah's crumbling foundation. She should be in a position to best support the mission of the team, and not the mission of individuals.

It Takes More Than a Model

Building a successful, high-performing administrative team requires more than following a model. The fact is, people are complicated, and dynamics are always changing. There are trends and stereotypes that are more prevalent in the administrative functions of small businesses related to role importance, gender, compensation, and creativity. The admin is pigeonholed as a helpful woman who is underappreciated, underpaid, and overburdened with boring tasks. However, there are some basic inspections that you can do to prevent, or mend, common issues in administration.

> Asking your admin to be more innovative or motivated without clarity and support from you is like asking a tree to grow in the desert. The tree has the potential to be big and strong, but it cannot will itself to grow.

Likewise, your AM Houses need resources and protection. When the ground begins to crack, it needs a concerted effort to bridge the gap, repair the damage or relocate the house. A periodic inspection assures your team that you are invested in protecting their houses. It's a proactive approach that will catch small fissures before they grow into larger cracks that threaten to crumble your admin's house. By being aware of—and proactive about—breaking the mold of administration and creating a powerful village of AM Houses for your company, you will elevate your business above the rest.

Next Step

By this chapter you have completed the Adminnovate Model for an individual AM House in Appendix A. Even if you haven't changed the way you manage your admin team, you've done the analysis to gain clarity on their house. You're ready to move on to Appendix B. In Appendix B you will do an initial inspection on the house you've assembled in Appendix A. This will give you a good idea of what area(s) may need attention to strengthen the house.

Appendix B is the Inspection Checklist. Run through this inspection checklist for your AM House and record the results. The checklist only has two options for each question. Each question on the checklist is either in **Good Condition** or **Needs Repair**. Any answer that **Needs Repair** is a possible crack in your foundation and requires further inspection or discussion about this role. Answering **Needs Repair** to a question is a potential indicator that your admin is falling into one of the admin traps. For any answer that **Needs Repair**, cross-reference your Appendix A diagram and highlight the area that relates to the possible cracks. Only you and your team can decide if this is a real issue or not, but any questionable area should be highlighted for your contemplation and clarity.

CHAPTER 10

the village

It Takes a Village

It takes a village to raise a child. Having three of my own, I know in the deepest depths of my heart that this is true. It also takes a village to raise a business. Your village will look different than mine, or than the small business storefront you pass every day on your way to work. Your Adminnovate Model Village (AM Village) will raise your business, keep it running, provide the support it needs for growth, and look after it when you're not around. Make sure your village is made up of people you trust and who have the vested interest, authority, and resources they need to support your business.

Imagine your village is composed of your admin team (be it one or twenty people), each in their own A-frame house. Some houses are larger than others, but all are strong and well-maintained. Each has no more than six windows. Some houses have standard double-hung windows. Others have expansive windows that give them a greater view of the business. Each house is occupied by the right person who brings the right capabilities and personality to their role.

There are walkways between these houses and there is a courtyard in the middle of the village. Every house has a walkway that leads to the courtyard and to other houses. The importance of these walkways is to maintain communication between people and departments. Some will travel these walkways often, seeking input and socialization from the village. Some prefer to stay in their homes. The importance of the walkways is to give each A-player the opportunity to seek information outside their own four walls.

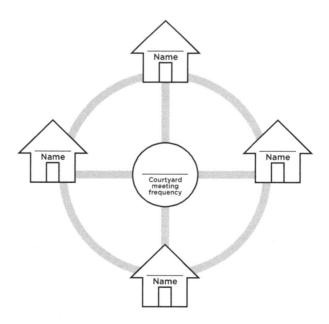

Types of Villages

On the two extremes, there are the villages that are over-maintained and those that are under-maintained. In this section we will explore each one and traps that happen. You play a key role in maintaining the village.

The Over-Maintained Village

The over-maintained villages are micromanaged. They have a central house in the courtyard that represents a manager living in the middle of the admin village. The manager has single connections from the manager house to each AM house, with very few connections between houses.

Melanie was a tenured admin at Nova Corporation. She embodied the qualities many owners seek in an admin. She was efficient, dotted her i's and crossed her t's. She was pleasant and always willing to lend a hand or train a new admin. She performed all of her tasks quickly and correctly. She had a lot to offer the team. Melanie was promoted to a senior admin at Nova Corp. Part of her job was ensuring all admins followed the processes. Nova's owner liked Melanie so much, she placed her into a central AM House, requiring all administrative information to flow through her—and demolishing the walkways between the other AM Houses in the village. Melanie's house was large and in charge, taking up all the space in the courtyard and leaving no room for collaboration. The other admin staff became resentful of her control and authority and frustrated with their lack of autonomy. Melanie was not authoritarian, but the owner designed the village that way.

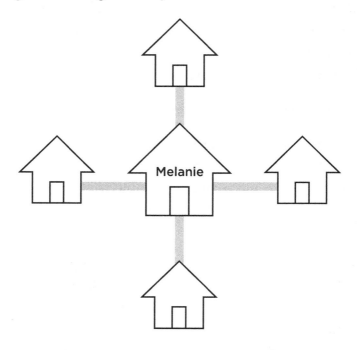

The over-maintained village is authoritarian and very inefficient. In order to get information from one AM House to another, it must go through the central or manager house first, then back out to another AM House.

The over-maintained village is micromanaged and eliminates avenues of communication. In Melanie's example, there was only one pathway from each AM House, and it always led to Melanie, radiating from one central location. This certainly ensured consistency—with Melanie's meticulous review of all tasks—but stripped authority from the other admins, leaving them feeling undervalued and over-managed. Over time, this erodes trust and opportunity.

The Under-Maintained Village

On the contrary, under-maintained villages have AM Houses haphazardly assembled with multiple worn paths snaking through overgrown yards to, from, and around every house. The connections exist, but are muddy and not well-maintained. People end up wandering from one house to the next without having a clear path of communication. The courtyard is a jungle of weeds, interspersed with patches of dirt instead of a groomed gathering place. This also leads to inefficiencies and ineffective processes as people try to figure out how to solve the admin riddles without clarity. The courtyard serves as a place to put out fires, argue over responsibilities, and sling mud when things go wrong.

Anne was the typical catch-all admin for Flux, a ten-year employee, and had a hand in all administrative functions. She kept the books, onboarded and offboarded field personnel, ordered supplies, and did anything the owner asked. In this small company, only two other admins were in the village, working in their own small houses, and filling in the gaps for Anne. Anne did not reside in the courtyard like Melanie, but there were well-worn paths to and from her house. The owner also frequented the village and used Anne as his central point of contact, circumventing the courtyard and the other admin. Without clear areas of responsibility, frustration escalated quickly when something was missed or done incorrectly.

The courtyard became an area for disagreement, rather than collaboration and improvement.

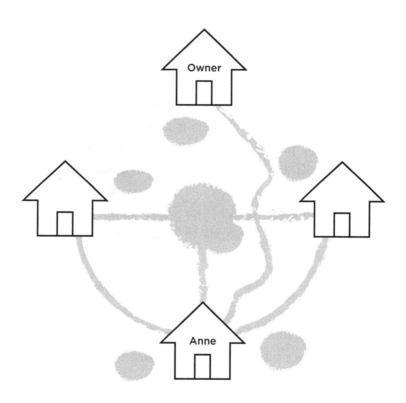

The under-maintained village adds AM Houses without a developmental blueprint. The example of Anne shows a business owner who hired an admin and leaned on her to figure it out on her own. When volume increased, they added more AM Houses to the village, but never defined their roles, requiring them to defer to Anne for direction. The AM Houses were ill-defined, allowing responsibilities to fall through the cracks. The absence of clear areas of responsibility made it difficult to hold each admin accountable. There were no structured meetings for process improvement or delegation, which led to an overgrown courtyard and tension between the houses.

Your Village

What do you want your village to look like? Every village should have three well-designed areas:

- Home Maintenance: Make sure each house is clearly defined and occupied by the right person. Make areas of responsibility and accountability clear.

- Build Walkways: Make connections between houses abundant. This creates a sustainable and self-sufficient village.

- The Courtyard: Make space for collaboration and improvement that is specific to your team. This gives your village the resources and autonomy to get things done without your micromanagement.

Take a look around your village. Are there any walkways that are breaking down or new ones that need to be placed? Did you design the walkways or are you allowing your admin to trudge through the weeds and wear down paths out of necessity? Does your village have a courtyard designed for collaboration and improvement, or does it exist as an afterthought? If it was put in place a while ago, does it need a little TLC?

Let's jump into each of the three areas in your village.

Home Maintenance

Imagine an admin assistant in a house, all documents neatly stacked on the desk. The windows are wide open, and as the owner or manager passes by like a tornado, wind whips through the house, the dust kicks up, papers go flying, alarm bells start ringing, and new information comes rushing through the windows. The admin is left in their wake, cleaning up, reorganizing, and trying to figure out where to file the new information. I'd love to tell every entrepreneur, don't be a tornado, but sometimes this is what we love about them. Innovative, creative visionaries can be tornados. They spring ideas on their teams, change their minds, and chase shiny objects. They are simultaneously inspiring and frustrating. If you're the tornado, don't stop! However, I will ask that you give your admin team some tools to withstand your winds when they blow through.

In the previous chapters we defined the seven elements of the AM House. With this clear understanding, we're going to perform some basic home maintenance. We're going to clean up some messes, change the filters, and reset the alarms.

First and foremost, clean up the mess. Most entrepreneurs started their business with a passion, or an opportunity that was unrelated to the administration of the business. The product or service was the main focus, and admin became a collateral duty. Think of the exceptional home baker who opens a bakery. The baker-turned-entrepreneur, has a passion for creative decadence. The baker focuses on the product and customer satisfaction. The baker is motivated to create beautifully decorated cakes and witness smiling faces as customers take their first bites of the sweet treats. The baker knows they must pay their bills, provide employee benefits, and publish marketing material, but the passion is in the product. As the bakery becomes more popular, the admin duties become heavier. As admin roles grow, they become messy, no matter how organized the entrepreneur is.

Cleaning up the mess starts with making sure each of your AM Houses are clearly defined. Even if you have only one admin, the catch-all admin is dangerous because:

- It creates a single point of failure.
- It leads to stress and lack of focus or innovation
- It stunts growth for your business and the admin
- It makes areas of responsibility unclear, leading to things falling through the cracks
- It leads to frustration when admin are added to the team

Using the AM House model in the previous chapters, define each of your AM Houses with appropriate workflows, titles, purpose, authority, personality, opportunity, and mentorship. If you've worked through the Next Step sections thus far, you have a good understanding of how these elements fit together within the model. You have challenged yourself to identify cracks in the foundation (as these are indicators of typical issues with admins in small businesses) and taken notes along the way in the Appendices. Building and maintaining these houses takes time and constant evaluation. The inspection checklist in Appendix B will ensure you and your team pause periodically to reevaluate the house and make changes. Just like your home, it will require attention every so often to keep things running smoothly.

Build Walkways

Building connections between your houses gives your admin team collaborative resources to move the business forward. When an admin needs more information about your accounting software, they should know exactly which house to go to and how to get there, without coming to you first. If all roads lead to you, you create a bottleneck. Creating paths to each other is a gift of trust and provides authority over their areas of responsibility. As the team grows, it provides autonomy as a team. It will create redundancy so that others can occupy the house—should its inhabitant take leave. Connections between houses should be abundant and clear. They should instill confidence in the team that they can find internal resources to solve any administrative challenge thrown their way.

Kendall was a project administrator with a strong AM Village at Hestel Construction. When her husband fell ill over the course of several weeks, her family came first. With little preparation, Kendall took time off to care for her husband.

While she shared the situation with her supervisors, there was little they needed to do to make sure her responsibilities were covered. The team in her village quickly traveled to and from Kendall's house to make sure information continued to flow as usual. Kendall could focus on her family and the company could continue to function as usual. The existing walkways were readily available when needed, and this was a situation where they were needed. When Kendall returned to her AM House several weeks later, she did not return to a mess or piles of incomplete tasks. She was able to pick up where her team left off.

Kendall's example might scare some administrators because they want to be indispensible. If the team can function well while they're gone, they may see this as a threat to their position. They may feel disposable or insignificant. Your admin should always feel comfortable taking time off when needed and not have the stress of returning to a mess. When other A-players can band together, this should be a temporary situation and is not intended to be sustainable or replace your missing A-player. If this feels threatening to your admin, it's time to reinspect their house. If having connections to other admin roles weakens the village, then there are likely cracks in the foundation. Walkways should only strengthen a village.

The Courtyard

The purpose of the courtyard is to provide a space for collaboration specific to the administrative team. If you have more than two admins, they need a defined courtyard. While they may attend staff meetings or one-on-one meetings with you, they should also have a space to meet with each other to work out issues that directly impact their village. Whether you designate a meeting structure for them or it's self-directed, your responsibility is to make sure it exists and is being maintained.

Admins will typically get into the daily grind of their work and allow the courtyard to degrade over time. They may not see the value in collaboration at first. Some want to keep their heads in their own work and not be bothered with the other admins' concerns. Your job is to make sure they periodically look up and out over their threshold, leave their house for a short time, and connect with their village.

A year prior to Kendall's leave of absence, her AM Village had strong houses and clear walkways, but was missing a courtyard. It was common for admins to call management directly with questions or have sidebar conversations with one another that were not shared with the team. This situation was perpetuated by physical separation. Some staff reported to the home office while others worked remotely from home or satellite offices. There were documented processes to follow, but each admin did things a little differently. Many hours and resources were spent answering questions, tweaking processes, and facilitating communication. Recognizing the inefficiency of the admin management, a meeting was initiated for the admins to gather virtually, report metrics, ask questions and debate issues. This courtyard meeting started with heavy facilitation by management. However, with time and structure, the team took ownership of the meeting. It evolved into a self-directed meeting with a clear agenda and resulted in action plans that strengthened the team.

The presence of the meeting did not eliminate sidebar questions and conversations, but reduced them significantly. Involvement from management was only needed when there were urgent or higher-level decisions to be made. All other issues were worked out in the courtyard meeting. In addition, the courtyard meeting gave an avenue of self-reported metrics that created a report for management's review. Workloads and deadlines were readily available to the company and updated at each meeting. Management did not need to spend time walking from house to house to gather this information. It was assembled and lived in the courtyard.

Your village may not be large enough to require such a structured approach to your courtyard. However, the more people you add, the more structure you need. If your AM Village is only one to three people, their courtyard meetings may be more casual and organic. Your job is to set the expectation that your A-players will come out of their AM Houses and meet in the courtyard periodically to review processes and correct inefficiencies. The objective of each courtyard meeting is to answer the questions of what's working and what's not working.

Without these periodic touchpoints to air out issues and build better processes, the courtyard will become an overgrown mud pit. When something goes wrong, you will be dragged into the middle for a mud-slinging match. This results in power struggles and bitterness in your village. On the contrary, the lack of a courtyard results in inefficient communication and overextended resources to manage the village. A well-maintained courtyard with periodic courtyard meetings is the proactive approach to maintaining a sustainable village.

While each company will find a courtyard meeting structure that works for them, I have provided a sample agenda in Appendix D (and downloadable at jamievanek.com/bonuses). This will give you and your admins a starting point for the meeting. As it evolves, you may find that certain sections of the meeting are no longer adding value, or you might identify a new section. The format I've provided is intended to be a living document and tweaked for your company's specific needs. The most important part of the agenda is giving each person in the village a voice. Resist the urge to dominate the meeting with your voice. Each admin must have at least one piece of information that they bring to the meeting, whether it's a metric, issue, or information. Start your first meeting by following the agenda. As the meeting evolves, make the changes one at a time. Items on the agenda that you initially deemed unimportant may strike a chord with someone else in the village.

Connected Villages

If your company is large enough to have more than one person in an administrative department, you may find that forming a single village for all administrative staff is difficult. For example, maybe you have three admins who are in the financial village, and another four in the operations village. The financial village and operations village each have their own courtyard, but there are walkways that connect the villages. Remember, your departments are not working in silos. In this example, your bookkeeper can visit the operations village and attend a courtyard meeting when warranted, and vice versa. As long as each admin understands where they live, the interconnection of departments and villages keeps communication strong.

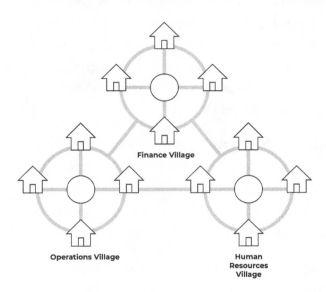

Having clarity and separation in roles is important from house to house and from village to village. However, the connection and communication between departments creates a cohesive culture, efficient processes and great opportunities.

Similar to the walkways within the village, be aware of neglected walkways or those who want to erect fences. An organization with clarity has no need to erect barriers. People understand their area of responsibility and do not need to be walled off from other villages. When people are clear on their role, there is no need to trespass on anyone's property. When fences are built, opportunities are stifled and motivation diminishes. Keep your walkways always open for travel.

The neglected walkways happen when connections between villages get muddy. When processes are unclear or inefficient between departments, the walkways break down. Information gets stranded and debris accumulates. Anyone who has ever been involved in inter-department rivalries understands the collateral trash that gets left out for management to clean up. Prevent this waste of time and resources and make village connections clear and clean.

Workflows that pass between departments need clear delineation of which parts reside in which village. We see the same issues that happen between houses, just on a larger scale with more horsepower behind them. Clarity keeps walkways free of debris, weeds, mud, and fences.

Your small business may not have enough administrative personnel to begin separating villages at this time, and it's ok for all of your admin to live in one village. However, you're reading this book with the intention of scaling, and one day you will need to revisit this concept to engineer your villages. The concept is the same: clarity and opportunity are critical to maintaining your village or villages.

Conclusion

The idea of the AM Village ties all of the concepts together in this book. Each house has elements of its own that set your A-players up for success. When houses group together in a well maintained, connected village for your business, your A-players truly operate as an exceptional admin team. The ideal village is made up of the administrators in your company, or interconnected sub-villages, with clear walkways for communication and a common area for collaboration. The walkways and courtyard are often neglected, but critically important for the strength and growth of your admin team.

House maintenance starts with a clear model of each A-player's house and periodic inspections to ensure it continues to stand strong against the winds of uncertainty, change, or the visionary tornado. It takes a concerted effort from leadership to be proactive about defining and refining the house as times progress. Walkways provide open lines of communication to reinforce a self-reliant village that resolves issues and answers questions that impact their processes. A well connected village, or collection of villages, require less day-to-day management and promote autonomy within roles and departments. Finally, the courtyard is a defined and useful area for your admins to collaborate and work out issues that impact the team on a regular basis. In conjunction with the walkways, it promotes a self-managed team who is efficient and effective.

When your company is running at its best, you have an AM Village behind it that is efficient, effective, and enjoys what they do.

Next Step

Each individual house has its own diagram just like the one you created in Appendix A. You do not need to complete an AM House diagram for every admin on your team to move to the next exercise. We're going to create a quick outline of your village for visualization purposes. Reference the diagram examples shown in this chapter. Using Appendix C as a guide, map your village with each house labeled and separate villages labeled, if applicable. Finally, look inside the courtyard. If your admin team already has a time and space for collaboration, write the frequency and name of the meeting inside the courtyard.

If they are not meeting on a regular basis, write "Courtyard Meeting" and decide on a cadence for this meeting. Will it be weekly? Monthly? Will you allow anyone to call a meeting, or must it be during a regularly scheduled time? I'm personally a fan of the scheduled weekly or bi-weekly meeting. However, this is your company and the dynamics may call for a more or less frequent meeting. It may call for more or less structure. You can determine the specific structure later. What's important now is that you write down a baseline from which to start.

CHAPTER 11

adminnovate model: bringing it home

From the Top of the Mountain

Two days was not enough for our executive team to hash out some of the big issues that would drive our teams and businesses forward. We spent forty-eight hours together in a beautiful mountain resort. The first day was spent team-building through fishing, good food, beers, and friendly cornhole competitions.

On day two we met with our coach, Walt, at nine o'clock in the morning on a shady patch of grass overlooking an expansive view of the Blue Ridge Mountains. The sun was low in the sky and a slight haze painted the distant mountains blue. There's nothing more refreshing than crisp, morning mountain air. We could not have asked for better scenery. The seven of us gathered our chairs in a semicircle around Walt's portable easel pads, coffee and notebooks in hand.

We spent the next eight hours deep diving into trust development, company culture, future strategies, and unpacking current issues facing each business. As we listed our issues on the easel pads, the glaring commonality in the issues was *people*. Some were good issues, such as preparing for growth by identifying our next-in-command within departments. Other people-related issues revolved around current employees—their roles, their personalities, and their attitudes toward the company. We worked diligently through each one as a team, asking questions, providing suggestions, sharing experiences, and ultimately making actionable decisions.

Bringing it Home

We could not possibly make it through every issue and as we boarded the plane to return home, the conversations continued. I settled into the seat next to my colleague, Ryan.

"I'm torn on how to resolve my estimator issue," Ryan started. "Ron is a great estimator. But, if I give him a raise, he will make more money than his supervisor, Celia," Ryan explained. Celia was a tenured admin who managed the estimating team. Celia's role required both management and administration while Ron's role was technical. While Celia had extensive knowledge of the company, customers, and processes, she did not have the same technical knowledge as Ron. The issue of Ron's salary was not an issue with Ron, it was an opportunity to evaluate Celia's AM House.

I shifted the conversation from Ron's salary to Celia's opportunity for growth. "What does Celia's role look like in five years?"

We discussed Celia's growth potential and areas of training for several minutes as the plane flew over the Blue Ridge Mountains.

"And what is holding her back from growing?" I pushed.

"She needs to further develop her understanding of our products on the jobsites." Ryan replied.

We discussed opportunities for Celia to take time on the jobsites while maintaining her current position and seeking other training opportunities. Ryan committed to brace her house and make space for Celia's professional development. It had little to do with the original question of Ron's salary. He could receive a raise as the technical expert, but if Celia has a growth plan, the issue of Ron's compensation is secondary. His ability to envision Celia's role in the future of his company and commitment to protect her AM House made it easy to resolve Ron's raise.

While Celia is a unique individual with a unique role in a unique company, her story is common. Through my conversation with Ryan, many common administrative characteristics were present:

- A female employee was the admin within a male-dominated department.

- The admin's salary was commensurate with admin, but was easily surpassed by the technical team she managed.

- There were growth opportunities that would benefit the employee and the company.

- The admin needed additional experience outside her office in order to grow.

- Opportunities were present for her to gain experience, but a leader needed to pave the way.

In one conversation we were able to step through parts of the Adminnovate Model to gain clarity on the role, encourage ownership, and identify opportunities for growth. It was a simple conversation that could have a big impact on Celia's growth and Ryan's delegation. Celia's growth would, in turn, help Ryan get unburied. Once Ryan could delegate higher-level responsibilities to Celia, it would free his time to pursue more growth opportunities for the company. Win-win.

My Personal Philosophy

Your admin team is the backbone of your company. They are not the front line, creating the product or service of the company. They are not the face of the company. They are the strength that keeps the company upright. I have a personal philosophy that a leader's job is to make others' jobs easier by creating an efficient, effective, and enjoyable workspace. The Adminnovate Model has walked you through the steps to create more efficient, effective, and enjoyable administration so that your admin staff can become your A-team.

Efficient

Efficiencies come in many forms, but mainly in identifying the right tasks, cutting out the fat, and trusting the right person to accomplish them with minimal oversight. I have worked in companies who *overmanaged* their admin team, assigning "babysitters" to manage files that the team was capable of managing on their own. This isn't rocket science. It's basic efficiency. By implementing the Adminnovate Model you will cut the fat and explore ways to become more efficient, getting the most out of your team's time and efforts.

Effective

An Effective team is not efficient for efficiency's sake. They are efficient in a way that makes sense and is effective for the team and the company. For example, it may be efficient for the HR manager to give a new employee a quick orientation in the form of a handbook, but it will be more effective to sit with the individual one-on-one for a personalized onboarding experience. The Adminnovate Model helps you identify the most important roles and tasks within the team to move your company forward.

Enjoyable

Have you heard the famous culture quote by Peter Druker, "Culture eats strategy for breakfast"?

You can have the most efficient and effective team, but if they are missing a level of enjoyment from their work, you've missed the mark. A team who enjoys their work, team, and environment is immensely more productive. On the contrary, a team member who does not enjoy their role can become complacent, less productive, and at worst, toxic. Your team desires control and ownership over their areas of responsibility. Through the Adminnovate Model, we've examined levels of authority and opportunity that will create a high functioning admin team who sees their roles as productive and enjoyable.

The Adminnovate Model is designed to reinforce the efficient, effective, and enjoyable philosophy of work. Administration should not be boring, undervalued, and unappreciated. It is dynamic and should be leveraged to strengthen your business.

Construction

I love construction. I love construction for its structure and metrics. I love construction for the process and the end result. I love construction because no two projects are ever the same, even when they are derived from the same set of plans and specifications. There are schedules and budgets, man hours and real dollars. There are defined project plans with defined teams and clear project goals. And in the end, there is a real, tangible, permanent, publicly visible product.

Construction is a fascinating and ever-evolving industry that has been around since the literal dawn of civilization and serves people in ways that vary from basic shelters, to military training complexes, to symbolic places of worship. Most importantly, there are people: the people who create the product and the people it serves. The most important lesson that I've learned through my career in construction is that **who you work with is more important than what you do**.

Construction has been regarded as an ole boys club. The typical structure includes an owner, back office administrative functions, field labor, and project management. It's easy to draw a line right down the middle between the field and the office, creating a divide within the company functions and culture. While it's critical that every role has clear areas of responsibility, it's tempting to throw anything that has to do with paperwork and organization at the administrative team.

When I entered construction, I had the unique opportunity to see it from a fresh perspective. I did not grow up in a family who worked in construction, or study it in college. I didn't choose construction; the world chose to place me in it.

If you're a business owner, or were involved in your company from its early years, you likely remember some of the confusing times of figuring out when and who to hire. In small businesses it's tempting to hire a catch-all person in administration and expect more of them across departments, with a fuzzy, do-whatever-it-takes kind of management. Whether it was a virtual assistant or office manager, they picked up the pieces in the background so the leadership could focus on growing the business.

The reason managing administrative teams is challenging is not because the work is challenging, it's because teams are made of people. No matter the industry, managing and leading people is one of the most common business challenges and topics of thought leaders, coaching programs, books, podcasts, masterminds, etc. The unique challenges in the admin team revolve around the stigmas of the admin role and stagnation of opportunities. Small businesses and entrepreneurs struggle with managing their admin because the admin roles are assigned with little structure. **The do-whatever-it-takes gusto of a startup is exciting, but the longevity of managing a do-whatever-it-takes team is exhausting**. People are unique and complex, each creating a unique and complex dynamic in a team.

This book isn't about hiring **more** people, it's about identifying the functions you need and getting the most out of them by creating clarity and opportunity for a team that takes the burden out of administration. Thus, getting you unburied.

Figurative Art

Before entering the world of construction, I studied the world of fine arts. From Rome to Philadelphia, I encountered brilliant, perplexing and beautiful artists who challenged my thoughts and talents.

"You're weird," my art professor once said to me. My very strange, aloof, kooky art teacher told *me* that *I* was weird. What?

Tyler School of Art, part of Temple University, was once nestled in an old-money part of Elkins Park, Pennsylvania, and regarded as a high achieving fine arts school. They employed talented professors with free-thinking, hippie ideals and intellectually challenging artistic messages. I once stared at a hole in a wall, twenty feet off the ground, trying to figure out why the artist had made such a small and obscure orifice, only to realize later that it was an inverted cast of his ear, inlayed into the plaster wall. The walls were listening.

There was always something about the human body that intrigued me. No matter the assignment, I found a way to fit figures into the picture. My main focus was always people. I painted a torso with a barcode when the assignment was to paint something from a grocery store. I painted human organs on a playground when the assignment was to paint something colorful. I filled a twelve-foot-long canvas with bodies.

Leading a company or team is not figurative art, but there is an art to it. The common denominator here is people. Whether it's the variation of skin tones on a canvas or the nuances of personality, people are complicated and intriguing. People at all levels crave validation and recognition of each slight change of tone that makes them unique. Your admin team is made up of people who bleed the same blood, but desire individualized valuation. They are human.

Everyone Loves a Shortcut

While you may have great intentions to provide individualized support, validation and growth for your people, it's difficult to do when you're buried in the business. I hope you'll find the time and space to implement the full Adminnovate Model, but have no fear! When your time is limited, I have a few shortcuts for you.

There are countless issues that leaders in small businesses face in their administration but there are six common situations that will benefit from the full Adminnovate Model. Each situation is paired with a shortcut. These shortcuts are provided for two reasons. First, it provides guidance around the model without the investment of running your entire team through it. They are shortcuts that you can use now and will slow-build your model over time. Second, you can run your entire team through the Adminnovate Model but will still come across some or all of these situations in the future. Even with a strong model in place, you will reference these shortcuts for future situations. If you address these situations through the Adminnovate Model, your team will be stronger, more productive, and postured for the growth of your company.

1. **Situation:** You need to add to your admin team

Shortcut: Invite them into your company with clear expectations of the culture and role. Use the three traits that you recorded under the name in Appendix A as a guide.

2. **Situation:** You have a catch-all admin person

Shortcut: Define their windows and purpose statement to avoid the helpful admin trap. Do this exercise with your admin and refer to the notes you took in the Appendix A windows and address to guide the conversation.

3. **Situation:** You're spending too much time doing admin tasks or micromanaging your team

Shortcut: First, take time to communicate how their role fits into the larger picture of the company. Then, identify areas where your admin can and should take ownership by listing three to five expectations of their purpose or three to five decisions they have the authority to make without your approval. (Refer back to the receptionist example in chapter five.)

4. **Situation:** If you need to grow or change your current admin responsibilities.

Shortcut: Refresh your understanding of the Producer/ Improver (P/I) continuum. Take the temperature of the new role(s) and of your current admin to ensure a P/I match.

5. **Situation:** Your current admin staff desire growth, but the path is unclear.

Shortcut: Provide opportunities for your A-players to learn and grow through exposure to other departments and/or mentorship. Under the key in Appendix A, refer to the mentor resources next to the person holding the wall and the list of opportunities.

6. **Situation:** Your A-players operate in strong houses, but the village is over-maintained or under-maintained.

Shortcut: Ensure communication is clear and abundant, with a collaborative cadence. Refer to your courtyard in Appendix C and begin holding your courtyard meetings. Structure the meeting in a way that requires each person to participate and facilitates discussion about what's working and what's not working.

While taking the time to run your entire team through the Adminnovate Model is most beneficial, it may also feel daunting if you have more than three admins. This is where the shortcuts can help to address your most pressing issue. While it's best to run through all aspects of the model for the entire team, you can take these shortcuts as needed. Since you've read through this book, you've gained the foundational knowledge and practiced the key exercises to understand how the model works. Over time, referencing these shortcuts will help your model take shape. If you currently find yourself in one of the situations listed, start your Adminnovate Model there. This book is intended to meet you where you are.

For example, let's say you have five admin staff in your company. You don't have the time to analyze each of their houses right now, and things are going fairly well. Your admins seem content and get the job done. However, you find yourself getting caught in the weeds of the day-to-day administration. Your office is an endless flow of people coming in and out, asking questions and seeking your approval. At times, you want to scream, "I don't care how you do it, just get it done!" You have the desire for your team to work more autonomously, but the habit of seeking your approval is hard to break. You are in Situation #3.

At your next staff meeting, take a few minutes to reinforce the mission or vision of the company. Be passionate and inspiring about why you started the company and where it's going. Next, bring the message into the admin roles individually. Start with your "go-to" admin who is mostly likely to help answer questions. Choose the admin with whom you have the most trust and comfort. Take time to contemplate the purpose and expectations of their job. Before meeting with them, write down three to five ways they contribute to the mission of the company and three to five decisions you would like them to make without your approval. You can always set parameters around the decisions.

For example, Dennis has the authority to make the decisions around the software used for timekeeping and payroll, as long as it costs less than five hundred dollars a month. When he chooses the software, he owns it—meaning he will train for it and maintain it. He can lean on the team for input and let you know what he decides at the end.

Managing your admin team takes dedicated effort, but pays in dividends once established. By following the Adminnovate Model Houses and Villages, you'll gain clarity in your admins' roles, see opportunities for their growth, and note ways you can unlock the potential within your company. Maintenance of the Adminnovate Model will also take concerted effort and time, but far less than the time and resources it takes to correct mistakes, manage miscommunication, and account for inefficiencies. Using the shortcuts and the annual inspection checklist, building your high performing admin team will become part of your culture and not an extra burden. The framework around the model is intended to make your job easier by making your team more efficient, effective, and enjoyable.

Wrap-Up, Parting Words

Business owners are driven by passion and focused on revenue to scale, but the internal framework must also be strong to support the growth. Neglecting this framework will lead to wasted resources spent fighting fires and overcompensating for inefficiencies. A solid AM Village will help raise your company to new heights. While we cannot solve every issue you will encounter as a leader in your company, we can construct a model that appreciates the individual and clarifies the structures for the benefit of everyone in the company.

I believe there is a stigma and stereotype around administrative professionals in small businesses. Through reading this book and going through the exercises, we have designed a structure that clarifies and empowers those administrators. My goal is to help you rethink the administrative functions in your business to dismantle the stigma. Implementation of the Adminnovate Model will lead to stronger companies and more opportunities for admins in previously pigeonholed positions. The talents in your existing teams can help build the framework to scale your business. There is potential trapped in your organization. You hold the keys to unlock it.

am house

Throughout this book you will be asked to do small exercises to help drive the concept of the AM House and create clarity, structure, and opportunity around your admin team. Use the diagrams provided here to practice the concepts in each chapter. It's helpful to diagram the concept to visualize each of your A-player's roles. Don't worry, each chapter will step you through an example in small, bite-sized pieces. The next page is a reference guide for symbols that you will find useful as you practice each exercise.

⌣ **FRONT DOOR**

🪟 **WINDOWS**

📍 **ADDRESS**

🎋 **GARDEN**

⚷ **KEY TO THE DEED**

🌡 **THERMOSTAT**

🔍 **EXAMINING NEW OPPORTUNITIES**

🚶 **BRACING**

Example:

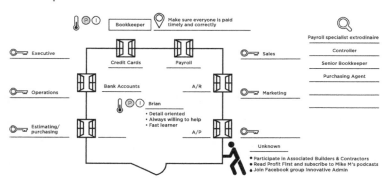

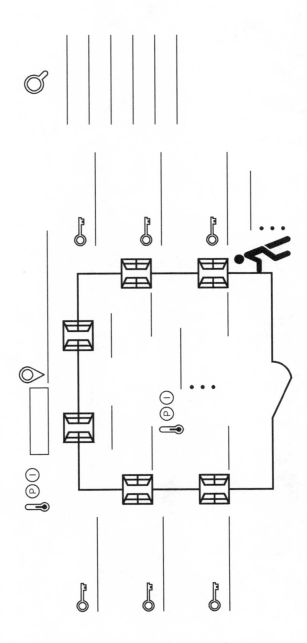

inspection checklist

Use this checklist as an initial inspection on your AM House(s). Then, integrate this into your annual reviews with each admin. The periodic exercise will help you catch small cracks before they threaten the strength of your team. Each question follows the Adminnovate Model. As you go through the checklist with your admin, be honest as you mark Good Condition or Needs Repair. Once complete, work through any items that are checked as Needs Repair.

APPENDIX B – INSPECTION CHECKLIST

Use this checklist as an initial inspection on your AM house(s). Then, integrate this into your annual reviews with each admin. The periodic exercise will help you catch small cracks before they threaten the strength of your team. Each question follows the Adminnovate Model. As you go through the checklist with your admin, be honest as you mark Good Condition or Needs Repair. Once complete, work through any items that are checked as Needs Repair.

	Good Condition	Needs Repair

WINDOWS

1: Are workflows and processes flowing correctly through each window? ☐ ☐

2: Including any changes, are there six or fewer windows? ☐ ☐

ADDRESS

1: Is the address still an accurate description of the purpose of the house? ☐ ☐

2: Is the address visible or otherwise communicated to others outside the house? ☐ ☐

3: Are there any windows that are unrelated to the address of the house? ☐ ☐

4: Are there any repeated violations to the purpose? ☐ ☐

THERMOSTAT

1: Does this house require a Producer or Improver temperature? (P) (I)

2: Does the admin person's natural temperature align with the house thermostat? ☐ ☐

DEED

1: Does the admin understand exactly what decisions they have the authority to make? ☐ ☐

2: Has the admin had an opportunity to venture outside their house over the last year to gain knowledge in other departments? ☐ ☐

NEW DOORS

1: Is there a clear path for growth in this house? ☐ ☐

2: Does the admin want to learn more about growth opportunities at this time? ☐ ☐

3: Is the admin receiving guidance from a mentor? ☐ ☐

DOWNLOAD: JAMIEVANEK.COM/BONUSES

APPENDIX C

am village

Use the pre-drawn AM Village diagram on the next page or draw your own with each AM House, connected walkways and courtyard. If you have more than one admin department, refer to the multi-village diagram to connect your departments.

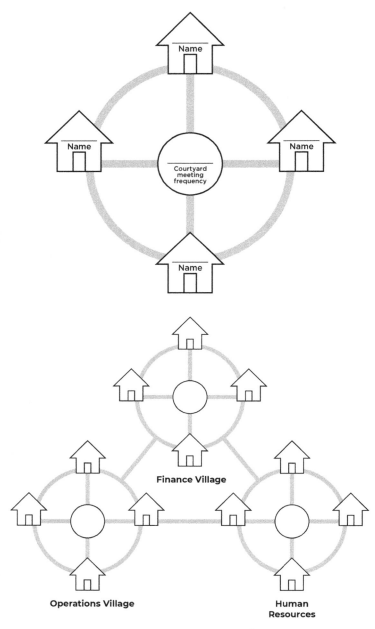

courtyard meeting agenda

The agenda on the next page is an example agenda for your Courtyard Meeting. It is intended to be used as a starting point and adjusted as needed to fit your unique AM Village.

HOUSEKEEPING
- Shut off phones, emails, distractions
- Review any internal house rules, reminders or expectations for the meeting
- examples: mute/unmute for virtual meetings, handling disagreements

ANNOUNCEMENTS
- Designate one person to handle company announcements
- examples: birthdays, staff changes, events, new projects

WORKING/NOT WORKING
- Each attendee describes 1 item that is Working or Not Working in less than 5 words

Name _____ Working/Not Working _____

Name _____ Working/Not Working _____

Name _____ Working/Not Working _____

Name _____ Working/Not Working _____

Name _____ Working/Not Working _____

- Once the list is complete, discuss each item in more detail and record action items

ACTION ITEMS
- Check off the action items completed from the previous meeting
- List incomplete or additional action items from Work/Not Working discussion

Name _____ Action _____

Name _____ Action _____

Name _____ Action _____

Name _____ Action _____

Name _____ Action _____

- Conclude

DOWNLOAD: JAMIEVANEK.COM/BONUSES

acknowledgments

No one expects to be diagnosed with cancer at the age of thirty-six. Throw in two kids, a deployed husband, out-of-state family, a full-time job, and things get tricky. As challenging as that year of treatment was, support came to me from all angles, and I began to see life a little more clearly. Big challenges didn't seem quite so scary anymore. Even though this book has nothing to do with cancer, without that experience, I may never have written this book. Thank you to everyone who braced my house during my cancer treatments, especially my village at the time: Kelsey, Brian, Mary, Jon, Jenny, Matt, and Tony, who wore pink friendship bracelets at work while I received chemo for sixteen weeks. Sometimes the little things stay with us.

Thank you to my husband, Josh, who supports my kooky ideas—like writing this book—without ever doubting me. You are a true partner and I love you.

Thank you to Cathy for taking a chance on twenty-seven-year-old me in the first construction company I ever worked for.

Thank you Cebert, Mike and John for taking me under your wings to share your knowledge and passion for the construction process and treating me like more than "just an admin."

Thank you John, for showing me what great leadership and mentorship looks like in both administration and operations. Your confidence and encouragement impact everyone around you.

Thank you Shawn, for challenging me and giving me the space to think bigger. You have a unique gift for vision and push me to think beyond my limits.

Thank you Kelsey for making me think more introspectively about how I lead and manage. Your constant curiosity and spark is inspiring to everyone on your team.

Thank you Russ, Shawn, John, Brad, Reuben, Matt, and Eric for encouraging and valuing my unique voice at the table.

Thank you Susan for gathering female leadership voices for informative, inspirational, and thought-provoking conversations.

Thank you Mary Anna for guiding me through the writing process. Your encouragement and accountability kept me going through all the doubts, curveballs, and frustrations. Writing a book is much harder than anyone realizes, and I couldn't have done this without your guidance.

CPSIA information can be obtained
at www.ICGtesting.com
Printed in the USA
BVHW041016300922
648380BV00002B/66